THE UNIVERSAL PARADIGM AND THE ISLAMIC WORLD-SYSTEM

Economy, Society, Ethics and Science

THE UNIVERSAL PARADIGM AND THE ISLAMIC☪ WORLD-SYSTEM

Economy, Society, Ethics and Science

Masudul Alam Choudhury

Sultan Qaboos University, Sultanate of Oman

World Scientific

NEW JERSEY · LONDON · SINGAPORE · BEIJING · SHANGHAI · HONG KONG · TAIPEI · CHENNAI

Published by

World Scientific Publishing Co. Pte. Ltd.

5 Toh Tuck Link, Singapore 596224

USA office: 27 Warren Street, Suite 401-402, Hackensack, NJ 07601

UK office: 57 Shelton Street, Covent Garden, London WC2H 9HE

Library of Congress Cataloging-in-Publication Data
Choudhury, Masudul Alam, 1948-
   The universal paradigm and the Islamic world-system : economy, society, ethics and
science / by Masudul Alam Choudhury.
      p. cm.
   Includes bibliographical references and index.
   ISBN-13: 978-981-270-460-3
   ISBN-10: 981-270-460-4
   1. Economics--Religious aspects--Islam. 2. Islam and science. 3. Knowledge,
Theory of (Islam) I. Title.
BP173.75.C493 2008
297.2'7--dc22

                                2007035459

British Library Cataloguing-in-Publication Data
A catalogue record for this book is available from the British Library.

Typeset by Stallion Press
Email: enquiries@stallionpress.com

Printed in Singapore.

DEDICATED TO

Friends and colleagues who uphold the
Universal Paradigm of Oneness of God
in explaining the Ultimate Reality

Contents

List of Figures

Acknowledgments

I owe my gratitude to Professor AbulHasan Sadeq, Vice-Chancellor of Asian University of Bangladesh, for hosting the December 2005 International Conference on the Universal Paradigm and the World-System, from which this book emanated. As a result, it is now possible to convey the Universal Paradigm idea to postgraduate students of Islamic economics and finance at Trisakti University, Jakarta, Indonesia and elsewhere.

A paper based on this work was presented at the invited lecture in Markfield Institute of Higher Education, Leicester, UK in April 2006. Thanks, MIHE. In this regard, my special thanks go to Professor Toseef Azid, who was visiting Professor in MIHE, and to Dr. Seif Tajuddin, head of the Economics Department at MIHE.

After my professorship at Cape Breton, my new position is as Professor of Economics and Finance in Sultan Qaboos University, and I thank the University for providing me with the pleasant environment in which to complete this work.

My sincerest thanks go to my colleagues, Professor Sofyan S. Harahap of Trisakti University and the Postgraduate Program in Islamic Economics and Finance, and to Mr. Burhanuddin Abdullah, Governor of the Central Bank of Indonesia, for their help in finalizing this manuscript.

Last but not least, I am grateful to World Scientific Publishing for the early publishing contract received. This enabled me to finish the manuscript on time.

Thank you all.

Masudul Alam Choudhury

Foreword

The development of the global Islamic finance industry in the past two decades has been remarkable. Yet, one can easily point out that the progress of treatises on Islamic finance and economics, for many reasons, has been somewhat lacklustre. This book by Prof. Choudhury is narrowing the gap between practice and reflection. It carries elements of earlier intellectual discourses on the Islamization of knowledge, and raises such discourses to a higher ground where the epistemology of Islamic economics and finance as a possible branch of science is being discussed. It is a masterpiece by a Muslim intellectual who has, for years now, worked consistently to sharpen the theoretical contents of Islamic economics so as to bring it on par with the occidental economics.

Underlying all the passages of this book is a challenging message that the strength of Islamic economics stems from the very fact that its foundation can be built in a non-occidental manner. Using the concept of Universal Paradigm (UP) as an operative concept, Prof. Choudhury provides an unapologetic path to the development of Islamic economics as a legitimate branch of science.

UP proposes a method to Islamic epistemology, in addition to "signs affirmation". Preserving the old tradition, the UP carries with it the notion that premises of knowledge should be grounded on, borrowing from Prof. Choudhury's conceptualization, the Tawhidi percept (which by the Divine Will is made instinctive to humankind), hence reiterating the Qur'anic notion that God is the Creator, Source and Giver of knowledge: "And He taught Adam all the names (of everything)..." (Qur'an: Al-Baqarah 31). With this, a Muslim economist can proceed with the ontological construction of theory and application that will radically transform how one will view the socioeconomic order.

In my opinion, employing the UP should allow the descendants of Adam to rediscover what they "had been taught" and realize that, like a well-designed mosaic, all the knowledge of God as spread in the horizon and themselves are interconnected and unifying. In the words of Prof. Choudhury, "the universality and uniqueness hold firm despite the diversity of issues and problems of interdisciplinary nature". This allows us to view the Qur'an as The Preserved Transcription (*Kitab*) that holds the key to all knowledge. With the help of axiomatic propositions provided in the Qur'an, mankind in his search for knowledge is then equipped to rearticulate the Tawhidi percept deeply ingrained in his nature. The end result is a continuous reconfirmation and recognition that God is The Unifying Theme of all existence and knowledge.

With this line of thought, it follows that the development of human understanding of economics should also be based on axiomatic propositions provided in the Qur'an, guided by the ingrained Tawhidi percept. Hence, economics is a positive science, rather than a normative rhetoric, about the socio-scientific order where the use of ethics and values when agents are optimizing are completely rational.

To end, I would like to congratulate Prof. Choudhury for this well-written and decisive book that I believe will set a fresh ground for transforming the current characterization of theoretical discourse on Islamic economics and finance, from being a normative discourse on reality to a positive science that truly explains reality with a predictive power, God willing.

Burhanuddin Abdullah
Governor of Bank Indonesia
Jakarta, Indonesia
5 March 2007

Chapter

1

Introduction

The Universal Paradigm is a study of the premise of knowledge that cannot be reduced any further as an episteme. It is the final core of all reasoning. It explains all experiences and branches of acquired learning. The Universal Paradigm is thus the epistemology of the complete, universal and unique premise of knowledge that encompasses all branches of human inquiry. The Universal Paradigm embraces all aspects of life. It expresses a concept of unity and relatedness between diverse entities and their systems spanning the micro- and macro-worlds. The Universal Paradigm presents a methodology that explains macrocosmic phenomena by a process of complex aggregation of micro-phenomena.

1.1   A Formal Definition of Universality and Uniqueness

A formal definition of universality and uniqueness that endows the Universal Paradigm with its special methodology is given below.

Let P_n be a proposition. P_n is extended to all numbered propositions n if the following properties of P_n hold:

P_n is proved true for $n = 1$.

If P_n is true, then P_{n+1} is true.

Therefore, P_n is true for all and every positive integer $(n + 1)$.

Furthermore, if n is a continuous real number, and if the above conditions abide, then the extended inductive nature of the proposition P_n is established.

In the case of complex numbers, the combination of the above two conditions of propositional properties for different forms of n is found to readily establish the universality and extended inductive nature of the proposition.

The quest for the Universal Paradigm of socio-scientific reasoning is to find such a P_n for $n =$ an integer, or a real number, or a complex number, so that the proposition for a given problem at hand holds true and is capable of explaining all forms of socio-scientific realities in the abstract and evidential world-systems. In this way, the use of the Universal Paradigm terminology and socio-scientific system conveys the meaning of the universally unique way of explaining all realities spanning society, science and "everything". The universality and uniqueness here hold firm despite the diversity of issues and problems of interdisciplinary nature existing in the world.

1.2   The Need for Propositional Universality and Uniqueness

1.2.1   *Economics*

On a simpler note, consider first the example of economics within the mainstream field. Its scope is defined in a limited sense. Within this scope, human behavior is characterized as being economically rational or with bounded rationality. Thus, the greater issues of social, moral and cultural embeddings that form a substantive part of human experience remain outside the analysis of mainstream economics and are treated as exogenous elements, which cannot be regenerated within a self-reproducible human experience. The predictions and scope of economics in its mainstream outlook, therefore, are almost always incorrect, evasive, unjust and inequitable. This happens because the primal foundations of morals, ethics and values are excluded from the economic calculus.

Furthermore, what is true of mainstream economics is also true of social and scientific studies. Just as the variables of economics in the domain of real numbers and integers are simply isolated from any parameterization of ethics and values in them, so also are these studies devoid of moral and ethics issues. Consequently, the universality proposition is negated in terms of extension and generality.

1.2.2 *Science*

Another example of ethical isolation which pertains to the natural sciences is this. Consider the Extension Problem between time-dependent and learning systems of wave motion: the sequences $\{Ae^{i\omega t}\}$ are continuously defined for different values of ω denoting amplitude of the sinusoidal waves in motion over time t. e denotes the exponential function with the imaginary argument $i = \sqrt{-1} =$ imaginary number defining the nature of motion of the sinusoidal waves.

As shown, the above expression for wave sequences cannot be accepted as a generalized representation of the sinusoidal functions, if perturbations are caused by a certain ethical induction of the parameters. Such inputs can be knowledge flows induced in the wave function through its parameters. In such a case of parametric variations of the wave equation, knowledge induction in it is guided and controlled by a given epistemology. Guidance restores uniformity in the sinusoidal waves despite parametric variations, and this allows for predictive power in such wave motions despite ethical perturbations of the parameters. An example here is transmission of sound waves. When predictive controls and uniformity are not established in the knowledge-induced wave equation, then distortions, loss of information and system entropy will prevail. We hear, but are not able to understand in the sinusoidal din of sounds.

Here is another case in point — the need for scientific controls and uniformity, for example, linked with the mathematical string version of wave transmission from a Black Hole phenomenon in mathematical physics. In the presence of uncontrollability and failure to gain information from the Black Hole, only mangled information appears from the string version of wave transmission.

The control, guidance and uniformity in the description of knowledge induced wave phenomena are specific physical representations of the wider domain of social and scientific interaction. The consequences of such analytical properties enable the study of equilibrium and scientific explanation in the midst of knowledge induction of the information parameters in mathematical string representations.

Such knowledge induction, which is epistemologically derived and then made to impact upon the structural relations of socio-scientific systems, belongs to the socio-scientific project of unity of knowledge. Whether such a project is possible in the prevalent worldview without the epistemology of unity of the divine order (law) — i.e., the Oneness of God — is a question totally shunned by the present studies of science, society and economics. The Universal Paradigm does not dispense with this fundamental question on the need for unity of knowledge. This central place of morality, ethics and values in all forms of socio-scientific systems will be investigated in this work.

There is much to be discussed on this theme in order to establish the indelible fact that unity of knowledge and life is possible if, and only if, the divine law is invoked under the belief of Oneness of God as the Creator, Sustainer and Cherisher of existence both in its entirety and in its most minute forms. The domain of the divine law and its relations with experience includes the hidden, manifest and cognitive systems of relations, and the minute forms comprise all those microcosmic entities which together define the large-scale macrocosm.

1.2.3   *Concluding on the need for universality and uniqueness from the examples*

We have stated briefly two examples — the wave and Black Hole — to establish the case for the Universal Paradigm in the sciences. These examples are intended to bring out the need for a new inquiry in the socio-scientific research program that is premised on the epistemology of unity of divine knowledge. The Universal Paradigm will be derived and developed in a methodological way on the basis of such a generalized methodology for the entire socio-scientific order.

Socio-scientific problems are diverse in nature, but according to the project of the Universal Paradigm, they share a uniquely common methodology. This is the methodology as it is derived from the foundations of unity of divine knowledge.

In Islam, such an epistemology of the Oneness of God, and hence of the divine law, is known as *Tawhid*. In the Universal Paradigm, the search is for a universal methodology of socio-scientific reasoning that rests strictly on the episteme of unity of divine knowledge. It subsequently brings out the functional nature of reasoned understanding, and thus the application of the episteme of Oneness of God to relational world-systems that learn by synergy between them.

The precept of Oneness of God — *Tawhid* — is thus removed from any metaphysical meaning, as in theology. Instead, the meaning and objectivity of *Tawhid* is unraveled in and by means of the cognitive and scientific representations in the form of laws, guidance and analytical explanatory power. *Tawhid* is not metaphysical and numinous in meaning and purpose. Indeed, *Tawhid* greatly affects the entirety of the mind, matter and soul in every detail, as far as the transmission of the episteme can be extracted, comprehended and injected in all things through the medium of evolutionary learning by synergetic *inter*relations between systems and their diverse entities.

The subtle limits of such relational learning are caused by the fact of incompleteness of knowledge in the human and inanimate worlds. The learning dynamics within this evolutionary world are caused by circular causation between the representative entities. The fact is that a foot rule cannot accurately measure the cosmic pyramid. There remains human awe and wonder, wisdom and dynamics in accepting limitations to know the divine law completely and to plan perfectly and wholly on the basis of such imperfect and evolutionary knowledge. The Qur'an declares, "No exact estimate of God will you get."

1.3   An Introduction to the Episteme of Unity of Divine Knowledge — *Tawhid*

Tawhid, as the episteme of Oneness of God in the Qur'an, is not limited by the material bounds of time and space. The Qur'an constructs historical processes by ancient narrations that leave a lasting and permanent moral import for the guidance of mankind and the applicability of the underlying laws, guidance and lessons for human experience. From the primordial "Beginning" comes the fundamental belief in God as One who is full of knowledge, perfect, pure and complete. God is alone, without intermediate agency in any shape, form and implication. Thus, the Beginning of God's Domain of Knowledge is a metaphor for the Open Beginning that is uncreated. Yet, it creates everything out of sheer divine command and will — "Be, and it was". This is the exogenous knowledge setting up the nature of the episteme of unity of the divine law for "everything".

The carriers of the primal episteme of *Tawhid* as Oneness of God (i.e., of the divine law) in the Qur'an are firstly the Sunnah. The Sunnah comprises the life, sayings and practices of the Prophet Muhammad to whom the Qur'an was revealed. Secondly, with the Qur'an and the Sunnah at the core of the primal foundations of unity of knowledge, the discursive mechanism of a participatory society is subsequently launched, along with its institutions and enforcing instruments. The purpose of this discursive mechanism is to exert effort in discovering the rules and interpretations of such laws, guidance and applications in reference to the fundamental sources of knowledge, the Qur'an and the Sunnah.

The Universal Paradigm will investigate these central elements of the epistemology, the ontology and the ontic (evidential) characteristics of the Tawhidi worldview and its emanating methodology for socio-scientific investigation and explanation.

1.4   Some Examples of the Tawhidi Application in This Work

1.4.1   *Abolition of Riba (interest) by social participation*

An important area of study explaining the functional use of the Tawhidi worldview and methodology in human experience is the Islamic prohibition of *Riba* (interest). The study of the theory of abolition of interest also leads to the understanding, analytics and methodology of resource-sharing in consumption, production and distribution. The interrelated treatment of these activities in the form of learning sub-systems in the framework of unity of knowledge defines a political economy with social interrelations between the systemic entities, in reference to the episteme of the divine law of Oneness of God.

However, even this is not enough. The Tawhidi worldview and methodology also fathoms the reasoning, analytics and inferences of the participatory worlds of matter and mind. These worlds comprise the seen and unseen phenomena that are investigated by means of pervasively causal relations between their entities in the light of unity of knowledge. The resulting emergent domain of rigorous study then comprises the social and scientific fields where the study of relational orders is primal for understanding embedded system realities.

Moreover, above the domain, there is the unity of knowledge between entities that is explained and measured by interaction, integration and creative evolution through linkages between them. The system variables are made to synergize with institutional variables in coming up with the configured relational world-system. The resulting dynamics is unique and universal for every facet of human experience.

1.4.2   *Circular causation and endogenous system relations*

The unifying learning interrelations explaining the system synergies by means of interactive, integrative and evolutionary properties of the relations are referred to as circular causation. The variables and agents of these relations as entities experiencing such learning and unifying interrelations become endogenously affected. That is to say, all variable-relations are systemic and are co-evolved through the process of their synergetic reproduction. The institutional rules and guidance and policy instruments are likewise endogenized by the social participation that ensues in the consequent interactive, integrative and evolutionary processes. A strong sense of moral and ethical values and a demand for social and economic change remain the cause and effect of the dynamics that inheres.

The law of interest (*Riba*) in the Qur'an and the negative relationship of *Riba* with trade, productivity, charity, spending in life-sustaining goods and the well-being so attained, together open up new avenues for socio-scientific re-inquiry. One such avenue of fresh intellectual inquiry is a thorough epistemological investigation in an ethico-economic general systems model. The theory of abolition of interest in the midst of the circular causation relations between the above-mentioned variables opposed to *Riba* opens up a new vista of the political economy of sharing via systemic participation of all kinds.

1.4.3   *Technological change in the Tawhidi worldview to be studied*

Another important application of the Tawhidi worldview relates to technological development. Apparently, it appears that continuously evolving human and institutional capability plus appropriate technological development can adequately address social concerns. That is not so, however, because technology alone is insufficient. Technological change must be defined and utilized in the broadest social sense of participation. In this sense, only a Tawhidi ethically-induced transformation of development capability and functioning is apt in solving problems that can arise from technological change. Comprehensive social concerns connected with technological change necessitate alleviation of poverty and reduction of deprivation and destitution. The Tawhidi transformation empowers, enables and entitles everyone with social justice, participation and equitable distribution of resources. We will argue in the light of the Tawhidi worldview that continuing poverty is the fault of human institutions and practices rather than of any inadequacy of physical resources, endowment and human expertise. In addition, we will show that resources and capability with social functioning are reproducible attributes in the framework of the Tawhidi worldview and its methodology and applications.

1.4.4   *Economic application*

The — traditional and narrow — definition of economics as a study of optimal allocation of scarce resources between competing ends for maximizing human needs and wants, becomes outmoded in the framework of the Tawhidi worldview and methodology. Briefly stated, the Tawhidi embedding of economics in moral and ethical values, institutional and legal, cultural, social and religious functions enables economics to truly become a study of the extended field of political economy and world-systems. We have used these attributes for the comprehensive understanding of economics, society and science as the socio-scientific worldview of unity of knowledge across diverse domains and entities (Choudhury, 1992, 2002).

In the conservation and reproducible world-system under *Tawhid*, in which past and present complement each other, the following attributes will exist:

(1) Normal science and the mainstream wertfrei approach to economic reasoning are replaced by a scientific revolution in socio-scientific thinking.

(2) Old and new institutionalisms are replaced by a totally different social contract with participatory systemic and institutional relations.

(3) The moral (i.e., divine) law predominates over all others, including the humanistic perception of ethics.

(4) The present conception of democracy as a political philosophy of power and hegemony is replaced by a participatory democracy with an extensive framework of decision-making wherein the discursive society flourishes.

(5) The idea and functions of a just society take their roots from the epistemology of divine oneness with its many analytical and functional implications for system studies.

1.5   Other Consequences of Tawhidi Epistemology to be Studied

This book will show that by the Tawhidi argumentation, the prevailing economic reasoning is changed altogether and replaced by a new one that takes shape and form in the Tawhidi revolutionary world-system according to its framework of unity of knowledge. Political economy will take its natural configuration within this kind of unitary worldview. Conflict resolution in every sphere of experience will be spearheaded by the institutions of a participatory and discursive society.

Thus, the Universal Paradigm in the framework of unity of divine knowledge can be uniquely appealing to people questing for truth. Good faith and true scholars, who remain on the path in search of the ultimate nature of reality, will find the new and revolutionary paradigm universally appealing. In so doing, such a global pursuit for truth in the scheme of things will unquestionably result in a deeply moral and intellectual lead on the way to creating a just and peaceful mindspace and global order.

The author has endeavored to cover the main aspects of the Universal Paradigm under the Tawhidi worldview and methodology. Within the Tawhidi epistemology, the Universal Paradigm will be taken up, particularly, as the study of generalized systems with circular causation and unifying *inter*relationships between the abolition of interest/ *Riba*, resource mobilization, creation of trade, productivity, charity, spending and efficiency and institutional structure of discourse and decision-making. Both social and scientific problems will be tackled in the comparative perspective of mainstream methodology and the episteme of unity of knowledge.

The book carefully studies the functional aspects of *Tawhid* in such domains. The approach here is thus one of political economy and world-systems as opposed to being narrowly thematic as in conventional economics. The latter remains separated from ethics, society and culture. It treats these values as exogenous, which means coming from outside the systemic relations. In contrast, our treatment of such values will be endogenous (i.e., growing from within) by way of system learning. In this regard, the book will study substantively the unified system's implications in the context of the total humanly embedded system constructed by *Tawhid*. Yet, the book will also maintain a comparative socio-scientific investigation in its intellectual pursuit to bring out the contrasts and the differences in applications.

Chapter

2

Concept of Worldview versus Paradigm

2.1   Types of Paradigms

A paradigm conveys the development of an altogether new scientific mindset from the old or prevailing one. It contains deep assumptions, concepts and values to make it a viable seat of reasoning and application. Yet, such aspects of the paradigm must have the nature of ready acceptance and appeal to all systems of thought. When the paradigm emerges, it pervades all systems of human experience including science and society, their institutions and the domain of individual and collective behavior.

When paradigms are segmented by disciplines of human inquiry, they have limited power to span "everything". For instance, Barrow (1991) and Hawking (1988) have endeavored to provide a paradigm as theories of "everything" that still remain far-distanced from the holism that the study of the total world-system otherwise demands. Consequently, such scientific pursuits have devolved into the speculative esotericism of theoretical physics and mathematical nicety in so many disciplines. In the midst of all these, even the very premise of treating the theories of "everything" from the limited vantage point of Christianity and Judaism left out the crowning role of Divine Oneness par excellence.

Marx was a victim of this kind of narrowed paradigmatic theorizing. Resnick and Wolff (1987, pp. 6–7) write in regards to Marx's overdetermination problem:

> Marxist theory, then, recognizes no single reality of absolute truth or epistemological standard that can serve to validate one theory as against another. For Marxian theory, validations occur within theories as they subject various statements to their differing criteria of truth. Marxian theory sees itself as one among many different theories, each of which conceptualizes its reality differently and tests its conceptualizations differently. Reality for Marxian theory is a totality comprising contradictions in theory interacting with contradictions within all the other processes that constitute that totality. Marxian theory specifies that interaction as over-determination. Marxian theory also recognizes, of course, that other theories conceptualize all these matters differently, they take different epistemological positions.

In brief, the Marxian socio-scientific viewpoint is that all the ingredient systems, problems and issues are differently conceived out of disequilibrium and conflicting views prevailing inter- and intra-systems. In such a case, the reach for the project of the Universal Paradigm is impossible, except that the Universal Paradigm for Marxian theory is the claim that the genre of world-system theories moves permanently inside bundles of social conflicts. The systemic totality here is marked by this internal movement within the world-trajectories marked by permanent conflict and disequilibrium. Within such world-trajectories, there is continuous recurrence of mutations by conflict, competition and disequilibrium of the entities, and their constituent systems, relations and theories. In the end, the Marxian view of alienated world-systems is one of "process" breeding "process" out of limitless mutations that never end. Hence, equilibrium, consensus, integration and stability of meaning and standards are not within, and cannot be conceived by, the Marxian program.

Thus, the limitation of Marxian theory is immediate. It fails to recognize the possibility of stability and predictability within limits of attained knowledge to organize society, economy and history according to the moral will of co-existence. Marxian theory neither explains the great religious events that span all of history without fading away, nor does it recognize the possibility of the union of nation-states and the reality of unification of knowledge in "everything" (Marcuse, 1989). Yet, the latter unification remains as the great scientific program of all time and the ultimate creative reality.

2.2   Thomas Kuhn's Structure of Scientific Revolution

Kuhn (1970, pp. 154–172) explains the differences between the concepts of normal science, paradigm and scientific revolution. Normal science is explained by Kuhn (p. 158):

> Normal research, which is cumulative, owes its success to the ability of scientists regularly to select problems that can be solved with conceptual and instrumental techniques close to those already in existence.

Paradigm is defined by Kuhn (p. 158) as:

> … universally recognized scientific achievements that for a time provide model problems and solutions to a community of practitioners.

On the other hand, Kuhn describes scientific revolution (p. 154) as one of

> those non-cumulative development episodes in which an older paradigm is replaced in whole or in part by an incompatible new one.

Subsequently, with the change in paradigm and a newer way of looking at the world, come about reorganizations and transformations. In such changes, new rules, institutional structures, human convictions and instruments to enforce the new ways of thinking arise. Kuhn (p. 173) remarks,

> It is rather as if the professional community had been suddenly transported to another planet where familiar objects are seen in a different light and are joined by non-familiar ones as well.

In all of the above, the development of scientific doctrines falls into diversely competing paradigms, one that Marx referred to as over-determination. Such differentiation and non-convergence cause science to be disparate and non-unique, non-universal in its worldview.

The project of the Universal Paradigm, which is premised in and then confirms the epistemology of the unique foundation of socio-scientific reasoning in unity of divine knowledge, therefore, cannot be part of the normal science program. Truth in every other scientific pursuit is infinitely and non-directionally reducible, following the wishful needs and perceptions of the observer. In contrast, in the project of the Universal Paradigm, truth is premised uniquely on the episteme of unity of the divine law. It is then prescribed and left to man to search, understand and advance along the path of knowledge and experience.

2.3   Worldview — The Project of the Universal Paradigm

The project of the Universal Paradigm as premised on unity of divine knowledge (laws) forms the concept of the worldview. On this matter, Choudhury (2000, p. 20) writes,

> The unification of knowledge under a unique set of universal laws that apply equally within and between systems, given the perceived differences in the specifications of the problems underlying the systems, is the essence of the worldview. We note then that in connection with the concepts of paradigms and scientific revolutions, the concept of worldview is the reduction of all paradigms and scientific revolutions to a unique praxis or theory. This core of all theories that enables the interdisciplinary systems to get linked up is premised on unity of knowledge. When the premise of unity of knowledge is identified as having vaster explanatory and applicative power than being specific theories to specific questions and issues under investigation, we reach the universality of such a super paradigm.

Boland (1991) writes regarding Popper's concept of universality in scientific methodology (edited):

> On the basis of the desirability of universality and precision, Popper (1959/61, p. 123) establishes the following rule:

"If of two statements both their universality and their precision are comparable, then the less universal or the less precise is derivable from the more universal or more precise, unless, of course, the one is more universal or more precise."

According to Popper, this rule demands that we leave nothing unexplained — i.e., that we always try to deduce statements from others of higher universality.

We note, thereby, that the search for universality in terms of a theory of the highest explanatory value and spanning the widest sets of propositions across the socio-scientific fields is the standpoint of the Universal Paradigm.

From the interdisciplinary relationships of any revolutionary paradigm and the non-cumulative nature of these great developments, it is implied that neither the reasoning of the natural sciences nor of the social sciences will remain undisturbed by this new way of looking at the world under the episteme of unity of knowledge. Much will change. Theory, methodology and along with it the analytical methods, institutional structures and applications, will all change with paradigm shifts as these converge to the worldview. The indefiniteness of paradigms of differentiated disciplines and the undefined nature of the epistemological premise of knowledge in various disciplines will forever be replaced by harmonization. Of course, interdisciplinary problems and issues will remain diverse in their nature. But the methodology of scientific inquiry and inferences in every issue of various socio-scientific systems will remain both universal and unique.

2.4 Is the Copernican Revolution Merely a Scientific Revolution or a Genuine Worldview? — Other Scientific Facts Questioned

Copernicus noticed the illogical nature of scientific reasoning in the Catholic Church of his time. The Copernican revolution was certainly a paradigm shift and left its abiding import in scientific thought of all ages. But was it a *worldview*? Can the substantive delineation of planetary motion by the Copernican revolution bestow on it the stature of being a *worldview*?

The Copernican revolution did indeed establish the geocentric design of planetary motions. It did not foresee the irregularities that can happen in this view of planetary motion. Hubble's theory is an example that has proven that, indeed, even the Sun is moving away from the center of the galaxy cosmos at high speeds, causing inflationary space-time expansion. Thus, in the light of the Tawhidi Oneness precept of the divine law working on the universe, the Copernican revolution was scientifically space-time bound. Such a picture and reasoning of the universe is inadequate from the Tawhidi viewpoint.

Another example of scientific inadequacy is the explanation for the transference of motions of fundamental particles as understood differently by Relativity Physics and Quantum Physics. According to Relativity Physics, the universe is in a state of expansion or moving towards a Great Crunch, which is an ultimate singularity. Consequently, the sun itself cannot remain in a static position under such elemental movements of celestial bodies. This is also the finding of the Hubble Telescope in respect to the geocentric movement. Quantum Physics, on the other hand, describes a world of scattering particles that never remain static in the probabilistic sense. Hence, all particles, including the geocentric one in microscopic high-energy movements, will displace themselves in every particular state of their configurations. Thus, Relativity Physics and Quantum Physics contradict each other.

However, the Copernican revolution and the Relativity and Quantum explanations have an additional weakness. The problem with Copernican revolution arises from the absence of an abstraction in the field of causality beyond the observed empiricism of the geocentric cosmic order. The problem with Quantum Physics and Relativity Physics is that they examine two non-integrated dualistic views of the universe. Relativity examines the physical laws from a large-scale view of cosmology. Quantum Physics views this phenomenon from small-scale sub-atomic levels. Consequently, the non-integrated cosmological views cannot arrive at a universal way of explaining cosmology, and hence, physical reality.

Abstraction is necessary beyond mere logic and empiricism in order to establish the deductive originality. Such an approach requires a search for the primal question of "everything". How can such a premise be uniquely defined, explained and made viable for and by empirical and transempirical conclusions? The answer to this question is essential.

Thus, the Copernican revolution, though being a paradigm shift with a marked impact on scientific thought, is still not a worldview. To be so, the Copernican revolution must be based on *Tawhid* (Oneness of God and the divine law) in terms of the universality and uniqueness of the episteme of unity of knowledge.

Pierre-Simon Laplace, the French mathematician and scientist, presented his great work, *Mécanique Céleste*, to the Emperor Napoleon Bonaparte, the philosopher-statesman. Having read it, Napoleon commented that the author had nowhere mentioned the Creator in this magnum opus on the universe. Pierre-Simon replied saying that there was no need to mention it so.

Two meanings can be inferred from this incident. First, the mathematical structure of the universe in the framework of unity of systems is an expression of divine oneness. Hence, the latter is intrinsic in the former. Consequently, there was no need for a separate mention of God when His supreme creation is made to reflect the majesty of God in the scheme of things.

A contrary inference is this. Laplace had no desire to worship God's handiwork. If this is the interpretation of Laplace's utterance, then *Mécanique Céleste* becomes a mechanical study of the universe in terms of observations and arguments, but not in terms of deductive abstraction of states that can be subjected to singularities and irregularities.

Thus, the Copernican revolution cannot be taken as part of the Universal Paradigm because of its silence in consciously invoking the divine law in explaining the majestic structure of the universe. Consequently, Copernican revolution does not establish a core uniqueness that can explain diverse physical phenomena under a unified law. This is the unique law of unity of divine knowledge, in relation to which the world exists and takes up its meaning. Such a worldview will be formalized in this book.

Likewise, the contemporary materialistic scientific revolutions in Relativity and Quantum Physics cannot be taken as the comprehensive worldview of the universe that explains "everything". The method-ological flaws exist in these latter days' scientific developments by way of truncating the general system-view of the universe into dual-istic domains. Between Relativity and Quantum Physics, the dualism is shown by their own partitioned views of the cosmos between the large-scale and the small-scale universes, respectively. Consequently, the universal reality seen by these branches of physics is different and difficult to unify into a grand unified theory of creation.

Furthermore, the laws of physics as so construed have neither bearing on nor ethical relationship with the human world. The socio-scientific implications of knowledge and reality are defeated. The Tawhidi worldview methodology found in the Universal Paradigm is opposite to the above-mentioned domains of scientific methodology. Tawhidi worldview comprehends the world-system in a comprehen-sible and unified learning methodology perspective of reality. This is unity of knowledge enabled by the methodological understanding and functioning of the divine law in the scheme of "everything".

2.5   Special Nature of Paradigm, Revolution and Worldview

The worldview, different as it is from paradigm and scientific revolu-tion, is explained by the Universal Paradigm in terms of the unity of knowledge. Indeed, this has been the time-immemorial quest for the theory and reasoning regarding "everything".

This assertion is the most widely accepted Universal Paradigm in all religions and is the ardent search by the highest scientific research projects today (e.g., HUMAINE, 16 December 2003). What makes the long-holding force of unity of knowledge to be reexamined under the new paradigm, the Universal Paradigm, is to cast this belief into a functional form of analysis that explains the widest possible world-systems and the process-oriented causal relations that exist between multidimensional entities embedded in these world-systems. We will articulate in this book the process-oriented methodology of the Uni-versal Paradigm under unity of the divine law as a rigorous analyt-ical formalism that is capable of explaining the widest domain of experience.

The call for scientific reasoning, therefore (Choudhury, 1989, 1990, 1997a,b, 1998), is essentially, the call to recognize the assumptions that underlie the thinking of the Universal Paradigm under the Tawhidi worldview and its functioning in explanatory systems.

This premise of scientific inquiry on *Tawhid* can be further marked by its cogent need for assumptions and specificity of problems and issues that are analyzed. But the foundation of universality and uniqueness, and thus of the worldview surrounding this, is inherent in all such studies of issues and problems.

The specialized nature of the studies is governed by knowledge creation out of unity of knowledge as the episteme. This fully characterizes the process-oriented learning linkages between all entities, either in the sense of their positive interrelations with certain entities or between those entities that get inverted under the moral and ethical law.

An example of a special way of examining resource flows, trade and spending is this — there comes about inverted entity-relations between the variables, that is, between trade and its inverse relationship with interest/*Riba*. The distinct method underlying all such analysis to be taken up in this book is marked by the unique principle of pervasive complementarities. This defines all learning relations including the inverted ones and between entities and their relations under the episteme of unity of knowledge.

2.6   Mainstream Economic Reasoning: Economic Rationality Based on Transitivity Axiom Criticized

The axiom of economic rationality according to Lionel Robbins (1935) was summarized in terms of the transitivity axiom between alternatives. That is, if A, B and C are alternative economic choices, and if A is preferred to B, and B is preferred to C, it implies that A is preferred to C.

In the case of the principle of pervasive complementarities formed by knowledge-induced linkages, i.e., unity by linkages between the entities and their interrelations, the following condition must hold: A, B and C being each knowledge-induced is an acceptable possibility, but all possibilities must be accepted in a bundle of choices, as this is determined by the existing relations that is discoursed among the representations of A, B and C. The choice then is $A \cap B \cap C$ over numbered interaction (i) taking part in discourse. Consequently, a well-determined choice is a complex integration ($\cap_j A_j$) over a series of discursive interaction ($\cup_i$) by entities (A_j), in any phase of their mutual knowledge induction. Such an interactive and integrative knowledge-induced choice is denoted by, $\cup_i \cap_j A_j$.

The idea here is that *possibilities* are not *alternatives*. The meaning of "possibilities" is that they are used as complementary events determined by discourse to determine knowledge flows. Instead, in the transitivity axioms of economic rationality, since A_j's are "alternatives", they are substitutes of each other. Hence, they represent events that are individuated by conflict and competition. Choices of such bundles are said to be individualistic. Now, when the same preference is extended from the individual to a subtle aggregation of such preferences, to the level of institutions and social contracts, the corresponding situation is characterized by methodological individualism.

Thus, we note the nature of the Tawhidi scientific inquiry in the two cases. On the one hand, we note the episteme of unity of knowledge explaining resource allocation and decision-making in the domain of knowledge induction by participation. On the other hand, there is the neoclassical economic case that *Tawhid* annuls. The latter explains resource allocation resulting from an optimal and steady-state utility maximization problem subject to the postulates of economic rationality, and thereby, conflict and substitution between the variables and entities.

2.7   Conclusion

Having laid down some of the formative critical background of this study, we are now ready to discourse the worldview as the Universal Paradigm. We will prove analytically that paradigms and normal science fall off the future of scientific theory of "everything", giving rise to the socio-scientific worldview. The concept of "everything" is not to claim that all issues and problems remain identical. That is ridiculous. The concept conveys the relationship that a fundamental epistemological premise unifies all diverse disciplines, issues and problems according to a unique and universal methodology. This is the methodology that arises from the epistemology of unity of knowledge. In this work, the concept of unity of knowledge is derived from the core of divine oneness. Divine oneness is explained in this work in terms of the unity of entities and their relations in systems determined by the continuously learning worldview. The latter is premised on the unity of the divine law applied to "everything".

Chapter

3

Unity of Knowledge as the Worldview

A new paradigm — as a revolutionary breakthrough with its permanent attributes of universality and uniqueness — has surpassing impact. It is the foundation of great minds and revolutionary feats in the socio-scientific world-system. By it the mind expands its vision step-by-step until suddenly, with abrupt illumination, it realizes its victory. Nations are moved by its newly discovered yet primordially existing truth. The awakening is as if a life-fire has come from the heavens.

3.1   Revolutionary Paradigm as Worldview

The ways toward liberation and coming into harmony with the worldview, now defined as the most universal and absolutely irreducible paradigm of all paradigms, are two. Firstly, it is to uphold deeply the indispensable validity of the Oneness of God in the universal scene. This will embrace both the individual conscience and the public order of all the sciences. It takes place in a reemanation of private and public activity on the scholarly, political and community fronts.

The second way is as Kuhn has explained — how scientific revolution is established. In practice, this way is to carry on vigorous activities revolving around the worldview by committed members, students, scholarly groups and the scientific forums that together ventilate the worldview.

The liberating effects of the worldview will then exist on three levels. Firstly, the epistemological level is primal. This will induce renewed awareness and consciousness in the beholder. The consciousness is that of beholding, understanding and applying the foundation of unity of divine knowledge to all world-system issues. Thus, the meaning of the divine functioning in such foundational knowledge is essential. This is to accept the divine roots of knowledge as the primal foundation of all knowledge, hence of all configurations of world-systems. Without this, in connection with the phases of knowledge development that follow, recourse to divine knowledge for worldly reconstructions is not possible or this remains a speculative enterprise. Divine knowledge must therefore be meaningful in its benefits for the broadest comprehension of reality and in developing verifications and inferences from it for the sustenance of life, existence, experience and beyond.

Secondly, the ontology relating to the epistemological phase, as the being and becoming of logical formalism of the epistemological ideas, must be articulated through significant scientific and public discourse. We define ontology in this book in an engineering sense, rather than in the metaphysical sense.

Gruber (1993) explained the meaning of ontology in the engineering sense as the reality of concepts, relations or facts premised on the epistemological roots. The concept of ontology as an analytical theory for determining *inter*relationship is used by scientists to explain the process of formation of such functional relations among corresponding variables and entities.

A definition of ontology that comes nearest to our usage is also found in Sztompka (1991, p. 51), quoting Lloyd (1988, p. 34): "It is the task of science alone to reveal the general, hidden, structural features of phenomena, and the underlying mechanisms of their becoming."

Thirdly, the epistemological (E) and ontological (O) levels must be encapsulated in capability and functioning. This functional level is called the level of evidences, which Heidegger (1988) referred to as Ontic (O). The emergent process comprises together the E-O-O phase of structured learning in knowledge-based systems according to unity of knowledge between their entities. Such a learning experience brings out the analytical, quantitative and empirical policy-theoretic study, followed by inferences, policy analysis and recommendations, program formulation and the like. At every point and phase of heightened consciousness in the Universal Paradigm, there is that indispensable relational causality between attained states of the variables and entities in given embedded systems. The role of institutions becomes instrumental in guiding the moral and social transformation in the preferred direction for attaining unity of knowledge by interaction and integration between learning entities and their relationships across various systems.

The E-O-O phases flow incessantly and continuously, as knowledge formation and its recursive induction in the systemic transformations emerge in the light of unity of knowledge as articulated by the monotheistic law. But at the end of every such phase of learning through the interconnection of states of the system under investigation together with institutional guidance, there comes about post-evaluation followed by automatic evolution (E) into fresh E-O-O learning phases to perpetuity.

The institutional post-evaluation of the degree of unity of knowledge gained in previous experience, which is a matter of simulation of a well-defined social well-being function examining the issues and problems at hand, charts the new paths of fresh evolutionary learning. This means that at the end of every learning "process" and the commencement of a new one, there must once again be the recalling of the foundational epistemology of oneness. The renewed "process" then carries on the subsequent ontological and ontic phases of socio-scientific investigation.

Every fully co-evolved learning "process" is thus completed by means of the E-O-O-E sequencing (i.e., Epistemological to Ontological to Ontic to New Epistemological beginning by Evolution). The recommencement of the E-O-O-E processes coincides with a recalling of the epistemology of oneness along continuously emergent learning phases of learning.

3.2 The Struggle to Establish the Universal Paradigm

Realization of the Universal Paradigm under unity of divine knowledge (laws) in the world scene and the socio-scientific milieu requires vindication of the methodology so defined. The methodology is further reinforced by its proven results and public understanding. The last one is a matter of enacting and implementing positive policies. The policy and institutional impacts commence best at fresh junctures of awareness, consciousness and education.

In all likelihood, the convergence of world scientific search for consciousness is bound to move all scientific and analytical thinking in this direction. There are already rumblings from the sciences against the reductionism of the scientific discipline.

Modern science has assumed a hostile climate of opposition to God in favor of materialism (Dampier, 1961). This must change by an accommodative will and vision. Hence, there will be a great role for positive discourse and understanding in realizing the great transformation to the Universal Paradigm.

In the global scene, the development of the positive socio-scientific thinking will depend on a wider spectrum of dialogues, rather than holding zealously to preconceived ideas of science, religion, culture, regions and beliefs. Thus, in this book, according to the dynamics of the E-O-O-E process worldview, we promote a climate of global dialogue between civilizations in opposition to the mistaken idea of a global clash of civilizations (Huntington, 1993, 1995).

Yet, in the end, it will be a fact that global transformation will be incremental in nature. In the worst case, this experience can ultimately end up in a bifurcated understanding of the world, with one side based on unity of knowledge and the other on linearly differentiated and individuated perspectives of socio-scientific reality. If learning of whatever kind is kept alive in all civilizations, then there will exist at least the impact of ideas on the differentiated world-systems to convert these into embedded and learning ones (Holton, 1992).

A great mind makes its advances a little at a time, not noticing the gains it has attained until suddenly, with an abrupt illumination, it realizes its victory. Progressive but powerful enforcement in the knowledge domain is the surest way to break down the rigid structures that clothe the establishment today and thus, to unlock the mysteries of truth. The Universal Paradigm is the worldview of this kind. It is enlightened by the unfailing worldview of unity of knowledge premised on the intrinsic monotheistic laws. The laws formalize the whole of socio-scientific thoughts and experiences, despite accepting diversity of issues and problems.

3.3   Structuring the E-O-O-E Worldview of Unity of Knowledge

As mentioned previously, the E-O-O-E is an intrinsic and automatic structure that is neither imposed nor concocted. It is natural and invincible to thought. That is because any thought must rely firstly on a premise. If the premise chosen is of unity of knowledge for the construction of the moral, ethical and social embedding, then worldly knowledge, life and experience must be premised on this very relevant epistemological premise. This is the meaning of Epistemology, the theory of knowledge that identifies and configures how a body of knowledge is derived and organized in order to address any set of issues, problems and questions within embedded systems with strong interaction between them (Smith, 1992).

The most important problem of discerning the selection of Epistemology is to find the law, text and knowledge that most universally organize the worldview of unity of knowledge. The question stands: can received philosophy of science establish the worldview of unity of knowledge? We will now answer this question from the socio-scientific and moral points of view.

The study of the existing body of knowledge of Eastern and Occidental world-systems shows that, at their heart, there is rationalism alone. That is to say, Reason is seen as the ultimate arbiter of knowledge, *and God*, though acknowledged for worship in many systems, *remains outside the human domain.* Even when a claim of socio-scientific and moral association with God is upheld, there is no means of cognate transmission from God to the world-systems to carry forward the divine law. Consequently, the reality of God remains subjectively dependent on human reason and perceptions. Thus, the primal role of divine unity of knowledge and its capability and functioning enabled by the catalytic role of a medium other than the subjectivity of human rationalism, remains impossible in such a subjective mindspace.

Such is also the case with recent thinking on complexity and post-modernist epistemology given by Giddens (1983a), Wallerstein (1998), Heidegger (1962), Husserl (1965), Russell (2001) and the entire school of economic neoclassicism and political economy (Phelps, 1985) and in the idea of science as process (Darwin, 1936; Prigogine, 1980; Popper, 1972; Hull, 1988; Dawkins, 1976). The message derived from all of these ways of understanding the origins of knowledge is subjectively relegated to human rationalism. The impact on the philosophy of science, including the moral law, the social order including economics and politics, and the natural sciences, saw the birth of a conflicting and differentiated understanding of human experience. The impact was felt equally on the hegemonic nature of science over culture and traditions and the political and technological domination over a natural way to pursue truth.

The politico-economic consequences of such ego-centered rationalism were many. They included, for example, the colonialism that governed and taxed the resources of India to fuel the industrial revolution of Europe. Marx's overdetermination epistemological theory likewise vouched for a theory of permanently disequilibrium and conflicting world-systems. Technology became the instrument of transference of the development, educational and political models from the West to the rest of the world by power and craft (Todaro and Smith, 2005).

During the eighteenth-century European Enlightenment, knowledge was understood in its material sense of utility and power. In other words, epistemology was derived from the ultimate premise of human rationalism. The works and beliefs of scholastic thinkers like Aquinas (1946), Kant (1949) and Hume (1992) reflect their incapability of projecting God and oneness in a functional and capacitating way through logical formalism, into the living world-systems. Consequently, rationalism failed to reap the subtle socio-scientific experiences of attaining well-being in the holistic sense of unity of knowledge.

A prominent dualism between spiritual and material values emanated from Kant's problem of heteronomy. Carnap (1966) wrote on Kant's problem of heteronomy as the dichotomy entailing the following kinds of opposites: Pure Reason versus Practical Reason; *a priori* versus *a posteriori*; noumena versus phenomena; the sensate versus the intelligible; and moral imperative versus the sensate world. All these became non-conforming opposites.

These are examples of the nature of dichotomy that marred the possibility of mapping the divine law and its spanning of relations into diverse world-systems. Such dichotomy came about despite God being revered by Kant as the highest existent and the source of the moral imperative. The gap in knowledge caused by the absence of a transmission medium from Pure Reason, the seat of the moral imperative, onto Practical Reason — that is, from noumena onto phenomena — marked the essential problem of scientific rationalism. Rationalism was opposite to unity of being. It militated against the unified and comprehensive phenomenology of knowledge. Indeed, scientific rationalism arose from Kant's problem of heteronomy.

Moreover, even the Muslim scholastics fell under the influence of a similar kind of scientific rationalism. The famous Islamic scholar and epistemologist, Abu Hamid (Imam) Al-Ghazali (Marmura, 1997, p. 107, edited), wrote on the problem of the rationalist Islamic philosophers:

> What is intended is to show your rationalist impotence in your claim of knowing the true nature of things through conclusive demonstrations, and to shed doubt on your claims. Once your impotence becomes manifest, then [one must point out that] there are among people those who hold that the realities of divine matters are not attained through rational reflection — indeed, that is not within human power to know them. For this reason, the giver of the law has said: "think on God's creation and do not think on God's essence."

3.4 The Structure of Tawhidi (Oneness of God = Unity of Divine Law) String Relation

Expression 3.1 on page 35 delineates the Tawhidi String Relation (TSR) of Unity of Knowledge as the total phenomenology comprising the E-O-O-E phases of continuous learning processes. Expression 3.2

on page 36 further extends the TSR to multidimensional space with knowledge induction of the emergent systemic variables and entities.

The following symbols are defined:

Ω denotes super-cardinal topology representing the purity, fullness, perfection and absoluteness of knowledge in the divine law. In the Islamic epistemological sense, Ω comprises the source of the Qur'an in its primal form of completeness.

Topology is a mathematical relationship that encompasses all forms of combinations of relations connecting things of the same or opposite type, including the limiting case of the total space Ω and the nullity, ϕ. Ω serves as the open cover of all its included sub-sets, sub-spaces and relations (Maddox, 1970).

Ω is referred to as the super-cardinal topology because of its openness and super-encompassing nature with the power to explain *all* realities through relations of such entities in reference to the divine law. It is, therefore, neither possible nor necessary to measure the super-cardinality of Ω.

The true, necessary and sufficient condition for Ω is to generate open sets of extensive relations based on the divine law. Such relations by generating knowledge flows that induce the cognitive and material entities and relations, carry the principle of pervasive complementarities (unification) most extensively over the sub-spaces of Ω.

Ω is never comprehended fully by human apprehension, because of its super-cardinality and extensions of mappings of relations. These properties of Ω convey the dynamic nature of the recursive knowledge formation and knowledge-induced relations between complementary variables and entities.

The measured veil of ignorance of human vision to know the fullness of Ω requires the mapping of quanta of knowledge flows derived from the divine law as the epistemology. Such transmission of knowledge flows contained in Ω onto the human order is realized by the existence of an intermediary mapping denoted by S. The role of S in relation to Ω is the key point of understanding logical formalism of unity of divine knowledge relating to the world-system. The continuity of the mapping of Ω by S to the world-system is contrary to the dichotomy between God and the world as in the case of rationalism.

We have explained that if S were to be premised on rationalism, that which Heidegger and Husserl referred to as Dasein, then human subjectivity will reenter the definition and derivation of knowledge flows from the source of reductionism that is sheer materiality and dialectics. As we explained earlier, dialectics marks a mutative idea of incompleteness and evolution caused by means of conflict, competition and disequilibrium. Mutation is also the brand of scientific rationalism. The presence of human subjectivity in the project of rationalism delimits access to the ultimate oneness as the episteme. Thus, in every aspect of Occidentalism, the role of the divine law as the substantive premise of all world-systems is denied.

In Islamic epistemology, the transmission mapping S must be of such a nature that it remains unsullied by human vagaries of rationalism. S must also be capable of deriving knowledge flows from the divine roots of Ω in a unique way. The result must enable construction and explanation of all world-system issues. Such a result arises from the combined properties of universality and uniqueness of the project of the Universal Paradigm.

S therefore denotes the guidance of Prophet Muhammad. These comprise the sayings and practices comprising the Sunnah. These are the only known record of prophetic guidance in the annals of religions to date. S extracts the divine law from the primal source of Ω by the medium of rules. The inferences are further discoursed, explained and applied in the world-systems and in human experience.

The tuple (Ω, S) thus forms the fundamental Islamic epistemology of divine unity, *Tawhid*, whose texts are the Qur'an (Ω) and the Sunnah (S). In the realm of mathematical logic, the confirmation of (Ω, S) by itself, as in the case of irreducibility of the divine truth of oneness of God reflected in the epistemology of unity of knowledge, represents the basis of its self-referencing (Godel, 1965). In other words, (Ω, S) recurs in every problem delineation and problem-solving across the widening nexus of domains and continuums. This describes the phenomenon of the transmission mechanism that we refer to as "recalling" of (Ω, S).

$\{\theta\}$ is the set of knowledge flows derived from the epistemology of (Ω, S) through discursive mappings involving conceptualization, methodology and formalism of the system upon which explanation and problem-solving depend. This is the phase that firstly projects the state of the system. The states are then studied and alternatives selected by institutional discourse and choices for reforming the state variables as needed, along the direction of systemic unity of knowledge as premised on and articulated by (Ω, S).

This kind of conceptualization by examining the existing state of things is the phase for the ontological principle. It leads to formalization and theory-building. In concert with our earlier definition, ontology here means the being and becoming of a body of thought and concepts that emanate from the rules extracted from (Ω, S) through the socio-scientific discursive process.

Let $\{\mathbf{X}(\theta)\}$ comprise mathematical vectors, matrices or tensors formed in complementary modes between the component elements as variables and entities. These determine the impact of embedded knowledge that gives these variables and entities their material meaning.

Leibniz (see Russell, 1990) in European Enlightenment and Imam Shatibi (see Masud, 1994) on the side of Islamic Scholasticism understood the concept of "meaning" of things in terms of certain forms of their relations in their domains of action. Shatibi understood the concept of "meaning" in the sense of extension of knowledge shared between entities according to their responses to the divine law. This in essence implies conveying the epistemology of unity of knowledge premised on the divine law. Leibniz, a firm believer in the existence of God, did not believe in extension of relations between variables and entities. He considered every entity to be independently endowed by its own "soul-like" nature and behavior, which Leibniz argued were primordially endowed by God in the entities.

In recent times, the theme of "meaning" as part of the sociological project of rationality was taken up by Weber (see Mommsen, 1998) and Schutz (1970). The debate on what constitutes interpretive knowledge has been waged from both sides. Those who pronounced methodological individualism, specialization and independence between the disciplines were led by Weber.

On the other hand, there were those who argued for a holistic society. This school was led by Durkheim (see Giddens, 1983b) and

Lyotard (1984). "Meaning" in the sociological sense is now translated in terms of making sense through functional relations between entities. This would explain causality between them. The kind of description as "meaning" so conveyed takes the form of translating sociological reality by means of signs and complexes. Such a field of transliteration of meaning conveyed through relations is referred to as semiosis (Heiskala, 2003).

In the epistemology of unity of divine knowledge carried through by (Ω, S) onto the world-systems, which are formed by the spanning of knowledge flows and their induced entities, the tuples denoted by $\{\theta, \mathbf{X}(\theta)\}$, form the domain of formal and cognitive existences, "meanings".

Within the principle of complementarities as the sure measure and explanation of unification between entities, $\{\theta, \mathbf{X}(\theta)\}$ are naturally designed by the divine law of Oneness of God in the scheme of *all* things. Such a natural design of oneness in reality is referred to in the Qur'an as the conscious worshipping of God by all entities existing in complementary pairs. Some of these, for our understanding of the socio-scientific order, are the variables and agents of the material and abstract world-systems.

Such an intrinsic worshipping is referred to in the Qur'an as the dynamic experience of *Tasbih* in "everything". The essence of recognizing the natural law of unity of the divine law in "everything" is referred to as *Fitra*. Thus, the world-systems, referred to in the Qur'an as *Alameen*, are continuously immersed in the worshipping of God's Oneness through their essence and in response to the primordial oneness of the divine law as the episteme that forms the unified world-systems. The laws equally explain the differentiated world-systems as contrary human artefacts of "de-knowledge" (ignorance).

Along with the conceptualization and delineation of the domain $\{\theta, \mathbf{X}(\theta)\}$ pertaining to specific issues and problems under investigation, also come about the formalism underlying the study of underlying thematic issues. Such a program for studying the world-systems on the basis of the Tawhidi (Oneness) epistemic reference reflected in the learning interrelations between the $\{\theta, \mathbf{X}(\theta)\}$-variables, appears as logical formalism. By the method of logical formalism, the law of unity is rigorously applied to specific themes that are explained by $\{\theta, \mathbf{X}(\theta)\}$-variables. The method of analysis in such unified and causally interrelated, complementary world-systems come about by means of circular causations between the learning domains of $\{\theta, \mathbf{X}(\theta)\}$. Such learning domains induced by the θ-values extend from simple interrelations to complex systemic ones. A mathematical or a discursive formal model develops at this first conceptual level, carrying the "meaning" of oneness of the divine law in reference to the primordial epistemology of (Ω, S). Such a concept of "meaning" in "everything" is carried through the discursive medium for deriving knowledge flows $\{\theta\}$ arising from (Ω, S).

The sequential relationships generated by topological mappings between the respective interstate relations are denoted by $\rightarrow$ in the portion of the TSR, $(\Omega, S) \rightarrow \{\theta\} \rightarrow \{\theta, \mathbf{X}(\theta)\}$.

At the end of this simplified one-directional causation, the objective criterion of well-being is evaluated. The method of such empirical evaluation is simulation. Simulation as opposed to optimization conveys relational learning that occurs continuously in the domain of $\{\theta, \mathbf{X}(\theta)\}$, where $\{\theta\} \in (\Omega, S)$.

There is a further refined relation here that makes only Ω as the primordial and S as the transmission medium interconnecting Ω with $\{\theta, \mathbf{X}(\theta)\}$, thereby, $(\Omega \rightarrow S)$ taken exogenously in the sense of "recalling" that occurs continuously across continuums of systems, causing the ontology of being and becoming. Ontology is thus the formal representation of the thematic problems of world-systems spanned by $\{\theta, \mathbf{X}(\theta)\}$.

Now, at the end of a specific learning process in the simulation experience, the simplified one-directional causation denoted by

$$(\Omega \rightarrow S) \rightarrow \{\theta\} \rightarrow \{\mathbf{X}(\theta)\}$$

is evaluated by carrying on the simulation exercise over $\{\theta, \mathbf{X}(\theta)\}$-values .

This is done by simulating a criterion function called the Well-Being Function, $W(\theta, \mathbf{X}(\theta))$, in the $\{\theta, \mathbf{X}(\theta)\}$-variables. The simulation exercise is done in reference to the circular causation relations between state variables, institutional variables and behavioral and policy variables. $\{\theta, \mathbf{X}(\theta)\}$ denote such state-institutional-policy-behavioral variables that are simulated to establish complementary interrelations signifying certain existent degrees of unity of knowledge between the $\{\theta, \mathbf{X}(\theta)\}$-variables and their circular causal relations. This part of the formal simulation model assumes an elaborate structural system. It is made amenable to estimation by statistical methods dealing with learning coefficients and perturbations (Choudhury and Hossain, 2006).

The above chain relation is now extended to the form:

$$(\Omega \to S) \to [\{\theta\} \to \{\mathbf{X}(\theta)\} \to \text{Simulate}_{\{\theta\}} W(\theta, \mathbf{X}(\theta))] \tag{3.1}$$

$$\text{Subject to structural set of circular}$$
$$\text{causation between the } \{\theta, \mathbf{X}(\theta)\}\text{-variables}$$
$$\text{estimating and changing their unifying}$$
$$\text{interrelations by computer-assisted methods.}$$

The bracketed sequence [.] in expression (3.1) forms a process of learning. It comprises conceptualization, formalism and a one-process evaluation of the entire phenomenological model of Tawhidi consciousness in respect to real problems and issues under investigation. The $\{\theta, \mathbf{X}(\theta)\}$-variables within [.] learn continuously and across continuums in respect to the epistemology of $\{\theta\} \in (\Omega \to S)$. $(\Omega \to S)$ is primordial, and hence, exogenous; but it is continuously "recalled" in the on-going processes, as shown below. On the other hand, the unification of knowledge gained by continuous learning across continuums of interrelating systems establishes the multivariate and multidimensional knowledge-induced relations. These are persistently of the endogenous type.

A particular completion of the simulation phase of (3.1) that closes a one-process evaluation by estimating the degree of consciousness in the systems, problems and issues under investigation, is called the ontic stage of the completed phenomenological model (Heidegger, 1988; Sherover, 1972). This part of the integral model marks the evidential phase in process 1. What is true of process 1 is repeated at simulated levels of $\{\theta, \mathbf{X}(\theta)\}$-variables in subsequent evolutionary processes caused by continuous learning in unity of knowledge over continuums.

The recalling of the epistemology of *Tawhid* (unity of the divine law) causing evolutionary regeneration of processes like (3.1) is shown in expression (3.2):

$$
\begin{array}{l}
[\text{Process 1}] \qquad\qquad \text{Evolutions:} \quad [\text{Process} \quad 2] \quad \rightarrow \\
\rule{12cm}{0.4pt} \qquad\qquad\qquad\qquad\qquad\qquad\qquad\qquad\qquad (3.2) \\
\mid \qquad\qquad\qquad\qquad\qquad\qquad\qquad\qquad\qquad\qquad\qquad \downarrow \\
(\Omega \rightarrow S) \rightarrow [\{\theta\} \rightarrow \{\mathbf{X}(\theta)\} \qquad\qquad\qquad \text{Recalling} \rightarrow \\
\qquad\quad \underline{\quad\downarrow\quad}\ \text{Simulate}_{\{\theta\}}\ W(\theta, \mathbf{X}(\theta))] \\
\qquad\qquad\qquad \text{Subject to structural set of} \qquad\qquad \text{Continuity} \\
\qquad\qquad\qquad \text{circular causation between} \qquad\qquad\quad \text{across} \\
\qquad\qquad\qquad \{\theta, \mathbf{X}(\theta)\}\text{-variables} \qquad\qquad\qquad\quad \text{continuums}
\end{array}
$$

The evolutionary learning processes of expression (3.2) along simulated new levels of consciousness cause refined concepts and applications of the $\{\theta, \mathbf{X}(\theta)\}$-variables to world-system issues and problems of specific kinds. Yet, this kind of evolutionary learning dynamics is permanently premised on the law of divine unity that determines the entire phenomenological character.

To endow the evolutionary processes with this character of unification, it is essential that the chain of processes in expression (3.2) must end up in a cumulative universe of perfect unification of knowledge along with the optimal values of the state variables. Since this state of the evolutionary system cannot be attained by optimization, under any condition, both in the small and large-scale universes in temporal order, the only possibility for the closure of the learning universe is for Ω to attain itself.

The necessary and sufficient condition for attaining unity of knowledge is summarized by the universal relation shown in expression (3.3). This expression summarizes the complete phenomenological model of the Tawhidi worldview.

$$(\Omega \rightarrow S) \rightarrow \text{Evolution: Learning World-System } \{\theta, \mathbf{X}(\theta)\} \rightarrow \Omega \qquad (3.3)$$

3.5   The Tawhidi Phenomenological Worldview: Tawhidi String Relation (TSR)

The necessary and sufficient conditions of expression (3.3) in establishing the complete phenomenological worldview as the Universal

Paradigm can now be readily deduced. The singular axiom of every problem discussed within expression (3.3) is that the world-systems are centered on unity of knowledge, whose epistemology emanates from the foundation, $(\Omega \to S)$. All other aspects of TSR are derived consequences of the Tawhidi axiom.

3.5.1   *Proof of necessary condition in the necessary and sufficient conditions of TSR*

Firstly, we argue by assuming that expression (3.3) is true. This is the necessary condition. The implication then is that the simulation of the evolutionary learning system cannot end in space-time continuum. Consequently, there is no optimum in any real-world problem-solving case. Therefore, only acquired states of the problem-solving system exist in simulation. These states are caused by simulation in given processes, as the phenomenological methodology substantively explained by means of the E-O-O-E worldview proceeds on in continuum.

Optimum in a continuously learning universe across its continuums of interrelating and unifying systems is possible only in two states that are unattainable by the world-systems. These states are either the instantaneous core of the system (e.g., theoretical markets, economy) or the ultimate two terminal closures of Ω (Beginning and End). These two ends mark the equivalent completion of all knowledge flows and configure the ultimate attainment of the optimal blessing of $\{\theta, \mathbf{X}(\theta)\}$ in the form of optimal well-being. The Qur'an refers to this Event of the End as *Akhira* (the Hereafter). The Beginning is *Tawhid* as primordial. The optimal blessing caused by such closure of $\{\theta, \mathbf{X}(\theta)\}$ is referred to as *Fauz al-Azim*, the Supreme Felicity. Likewise, the same kind of optimality is extant in primal creation. That is in the unity of the divine law. The Qur'an calls this state the Event of the Beginning. The primordial states in the Beginning and the End are equivalent and are therefore both denoted by Ω.

In the first case, the case of instantaneous optimality is impossible and meaningless, for in the state of continuous learning across matter-mind domains of reality, we cannot hold any interacting relation to remain constant. Quantum Physics has proven this fact for the sub-atomic worlds.

The other case is of the cumulative state of the End as for the case of the primordial state of the Beginning. By definition of the Hereafter in optimization calculus, the dimension of Ω now becomes super-cardinal. This denotes the dimensionality of the primal Ω, which is actualized in the Hereafter. Consequently, only relations between attained $\{\theta, X(\theta)\}$-values are possible only in the continuums between the two terminal states. No further evolution can occur in the two equivalent super-cardinal states of Ω. Therefore, $W(.)$ is optimized only by the completion of knowledge in the super-cardinal domain of Ω equivalently at the End and the Beginning.

3.5.2 *Proof of sufficiency condition in the necessary and sufficient conditions of TSR*

To prove the sufficiency case, we argue as follows: Let there be a tuple $\{\theta, X(\theta)\}$ belonging to the TSR (expression (3.3). Then, such a tuple is governed by the divine law of unity of knowledge. All the simulation conditions apply.

If possible now, let a process-based simulation state end prior to Ω of the Hereafter (= Primal). Then an optimum for $W(.)$ is attainable given the simulation relations. Consequently, Ω remains unrealized at the End. Likewise, Ω remains undefined in the Beginning, since expression (3.3) is then open with respect to Ω at the End. A truncation is now required to define the tuple $\{\theta, X(\theta)\}$ in respect to optimizing $W(.)$ within a truncated domain governed by expression (3.3) and not including Ω in the Beginning and the End. Now $\{\theta, X(\theta)\}$ cannot be well-defined within expression (3.3), as given. We arrive at a contradiction. Therefore, in order for $\{\theta, X(\theta)\}$ to exist with respect to expression (3.3), the TSR must be attained.

3.5.3 *Properties of the E-O-O-E Tawhidi structure in learning models*

The process-oriented continuity of expression (3.2) completes the E-O-O-E Tawhidi model of unity of the divine law (unity of knowledge). There are a number of critical properties of learning in the interrelations of the circular causation structural relations of expression (3.2). We now explain these properties of evolutionary learning in unity of knowledge. We refer to expression (3.2).

$\{\theta, \mathbf{X}(\theta)\}$-variables in various mathematical definitions represent the multidimensional tuple combining state variables and institutional and behavioral variables. This combination necessitates that the tuple is formed by extensive discourse (Interaction) between the worshipping impulses (*Tasbih*) of the socio-scientific systems and the institutional-behavioral agencies.

The method towards attaining a final determination of consensus (Integration) to realize a limiting value of knowledge flows emanating from the discursive sequences of knowledge flows in any given learning and evaluation process goes through institutional discourse to derive such a limiting knowledge-flow value. Limiting knowledge flows across evolutionary processes indicate levels of attained consciousness in the understanding of the rules derived from the epistemology of (Ω, S). The process-based evolution of the knowledge flows, and thereby, of their induced variables, simulates the Social Well-Being Criterion to higher levels of relational unity. This is to say that the system attains higher stages of consciousness derived from the divine law of unity of knowledge.

Simulation of the Social Well-Being Criterion under conditions of circular causation relations between the interacting variables now sets the evaluative point of the E-O-O-E learning processes. The circular causation between the variables of the Social Well-Being Criterion implies the relational dynamics between the $\{\theta, \mathbf{X}(\theta)\}$-variables for attaining higher levels of consciousness in the systemic unity of knowledge. The simulation method helps to transform an existing imperfect system into a more unified one. This stage gives the ontic (evidential) study connected with the knowledge-based simulation problem.

Up to the point of enacting logical formalism for evaluating the Social Well-Being Criterion, we attain Interaction leading to Integration in the learning process. These occur in response to the simulation of knowledge flows premised on (Ω, S). They are derived by the discursive learning dynamics. Subsequent to every process of learning involving Interaction leading to Integration, there emerges fresh learning along evolutionary phases of the same type. Such phases continuously repeat the processual experience of gaining unity of knowledge by transforming the systemic relations into more unified ones across continuums.

Hence, the properties of learning in Tawhidi epistemology are Interaction (I) leading to Integration (I) leading to Evolution (E) — hence, IIE. These properties characterize all learning processes of unity of knowledge. The processes exist in continuums of continuously learning variables and entities. These properties of learning apply to all kinds of socio-scientific world-systems in view of the proposition of universality and uniqueness of the Universal Paradigm mentioned in Chapter 1.

Consequently, systemic unification on the basis of unity of divine knowledge is universally characterized by IIE-processes. The Tawhidi worldview in its complete phenomenological form now results in the IIE-process-based methodology.

The final delineation of the IIE-processes in view of the E-O-O-E parts of the TSR is this:

$$\text{Epistemology (E)} \rightarrow \text{Ontology (O)} \rightarrow \text{Ontic (O)} \rightarrow \text{Evolutionary (E)}$$

Non-Process Exogeneity	Process-Based Endogeneity by Learning	
$(\Omega, S) \quad \rightarrow$	$\{\theta, \mathbf{X}(\theta)\} \rightarrow \text{Evaluation} \rightarrow \text{Continuity}$	(3.4)
	Interactive, Integrative and Evolutionary Field (IIE)	

3.6   Characterizing the Project of the Universal Paradigm in TSR

The project of phenomenology as the study of consciousness reaches its ultimate height in an overarching knowledge enterprise when it attains its unique capability to deliver certain principal prospects. These comprise capability to generate well-defined laws, rules, relations and inferences premised on the most irreducible foundation of Oneness of God (unity of knowledge).

The proof of such a methodological irreducibility follows the principle of self-referencing (Choudhury, 2002). The project must be capable of the widest possible coverage to apply its methodology, which we have claimed is the worldview. Also, the same unique worldview methodology must address both the positive knowledge framework as well as the negative "de-knowledge" framework. This signifies, as we have explained earlier, that the "meaning" of Truth and False-hood both ensue from the same unique and irreducible epistemology of *Tawhid*. The above points are clearly proven by the TSR.

Self-referencing is proven by the fact that continuing processes in expression (3.2) repeat the entire evolutionary learning process in the form of reflexive interrelationships between deductive and inductive reasoning involving circular causation between the variables. The epistemology of unity of knowledge premises the seat of laws, rules and behavioral traits on the specific texts (Ω, S). These are subjected to interpretation in a discursive medium.

Interpretation of the rules derived from the texts is done by the discursive medium called the *Shura*. The learning process of the *Shura* is equivalent to the IIE-process. The two equivalently use the method of interaction and integration (*Ijtihad*, search to reach consensus = *Ijma*). The same method of primal reference to the Tawhidi epistemology, its irreducibility and inferences derived from there by the interpretive experience, forms the core and periphery, respectively, of the Shari'ah (Islamic Law).

Extensive application of the Tawhidi worldview methodology is gained by realization of the entire E-O-O-E process. The polity-theoretic perspective of such an experience measures the learning dynamics in unity of knowledge using circular causation at the ontic stage of quantification of the variables and their relations. Such a method arising from the TSR is applicable to an increasing range of socio-scientific concepts, models, issues and problems, as the TSR continues to provide the necessary and sufficient conditions of deductive and inductive reasoning.

3.7   A Brief Reference to "De-knowledge Dynamics" According to TSR

The explanation of "de-knowledge" (Choudhury, 2000) is done in the same way as for knowledge. Though in this case, rationalism, methodological individualism and Darwinian kind of mutation between locally limited interacting entities, lead to bundles of bifurcated forms. Now, the totality that drives the "de-knowledge" domain in respect of specific issues, problems and concepts comprise continuously bifurcating relations between entities. In reference to the Tawhidi worldview, such kinds of properties of differentiated world-systems and their specific concepts, problems and issues are well-defined by the divine law. Qur'anic law explains "de-knowledge" as Falsehood. It denies the Signs of God as manifested by pervasive complementarities in terms of the Qur'anic principle of pairs.

The Qur'an mentions three categories of natural impulses — Truth, Falsehood and Indeterminateness. These are further explicated by the Sunnah. Some of the verses of the Qur'an clearly state what is recommended and what is forbidden. These bring out the differences between truth and falsehood clearly. Some verses are silent on specific instances. Now, well-defined determination between Truth and Falsehood comes about by studying the issues along the TSR. Learning processes that establish the complementary relations in the light of the law of unity of knowledge are categorized as truth. Those processes that differentiate knowledge, systems, variables and entities are categorized as falsehood. Such a process of deciphering between truth and falsehood remains incessant in continuum.

3.8 Conclusion

The worldview of the Universal Paradigm and its TSR methodology were developed in this chapter in the framework of unity of divine knowledge (law). In the Islamic case, the Universal Paradigm is premised on the epistemology of *Tawhid* as the worldview. This chapter has brought out this methodology and its details in the form of the TSR.

The chapter has also proved how the Tawhidi worldview is a supra-revolutionary doctrine, and thereby, the worldview. In this direction of establishing the Tawhidi worldview as the Universal Paradigm, a comparative and contrasting examination of other epistemological ideas in socio-scientific thought were examined.

Critical examination of these ideas led to the investigation on why and how the Tawhidi worldview stands out as the Universal Paradigm in the sense of the worldview. The concept of worldview was substantively explained in contrast to normal science, paradigm and scientific revolution.

Chapter

4

Human Consciousness

4.1 Further Topics in Epistemology

This chapter is an inquiry into further issues relating to the theme of epistemology. Epistemology is the study of the methods and groundwork for a rational understanding of scientific truth. Epistemology has always grounded paradigm shift and revolutionary scientific thought. They are also to be found to underlie testable scientific facts.

Popper argued along these lines, claiming that the best of scientific theory is the one that withstands the strictest testability and attempts to falsify it. He also claimed that for a theory to be scientific, it must be testable and thus accept the possibility of conjecture and refutation (Popper, 1972).

The subject of theology as perceived in Western science needs to be taken up with that of epistemology. Russell (1990, p. 13) explains the nature of theology: "All definite knowledge — so I should contend — belongs to science; all dogma as to what surpasses definite knowledge belongs to theology. But between theology and science there is a No

Man's Land, exposed to attack from both sides; this no man's land is philosophy."

The groundwork of epistemology may be either subjective in nature or substantively analytical. Theological premises of epistemological doctrinaire are subjective in nature as the subject matter of this discipline is based on claims like the nature of God in human beliefs, history, cultures and civilizations. These lead to simple descriptive writings without analytical content. The analytical construction of thought, methodology, inferences, applications and verification for the benefit of individual and society, as in the questions pertaining to world-systems and political economy, remain unfamiliar to the discipline of theology. Theological knowledge in Western context remains a study in idealism and historical narratives defying testability.

Examples of the subjective nature of theological foundations of epistemic thought can be found in the early Greek civilization. The Greeks considered the world and its entities to be driven by the presence of demigods in them. Pantheism thus narrowed down the domain of God to the material worlds of mind, matter and forms. This limited scope of epistemology rested in the narrow confines of the demigods, while claiming that the spirit of God rested in the supreme creator.

Spinoza (Koistinen and Biro, 2002) conceptualized God as the ultimate being but failed to bring God into the analytical constructs of reason and functionalism. This was equally true of Kant's heteronomy (Choudhury, 1997b) that divided the moral imperative of the *a priori* pure reason from the *a posteriori* domain of practical reason.

The relationship of the divine law, although upheld by Kant, was dysfunctional in mapping its relational functions with the world-systems. Like the ideas of Kant and Spinoza, Western civilization is marked by Hegelian dialectics. In this, the notion of the Absolute as the World Spirit is equated solely with the ultimate power of rationalism and reason. Hegelian philosophy of history is thereby reduced to the temporal world-systems of perfection and error in reasoning with the metaphysical craving for the perfect society that grows out of contradiction between truth and error. Yet, the lawgiver in this search is Reason and not the functional domain of the divine law that constructs the mind, matter and logic.

Indeed, Occidentalism is thoroughly imbued with this kind of contradiction between God's ultimate domain of creatorship that remains non-functional in the realm of analytical reasoning, and explanation. For example, Aristotle and Parmenides, whose ideas have profoundly influenced Western thought, are opposite exponents of the ultimate nature of the Occidental belief on the rationality concept of "unity".

Aristotle thought of "unity" of being not in terms of essence and the universal, but in terms of form and matter. The concept of divine unity was upheld. But it was thought to be imported into matter and form by the presence of demigods. This is rationalist speculation and contrary to the functional mapping of the divine law into the precept of "unity" in world-systems.

Contrastedly, Parmenides thought of existence in terms of imagination and phenomena in terms of perception. Consequently, development by form and matter as with Aristotle was an illusive matter to Parmenides. Only abstraction mattered, and development remained a delusive phantom. The precept of "unity" of being in the ontological sense was a restive and unchanging principle for the experiential world speculated by Parmenides. This is contrary to the evolutionary changing and agency concept of "unity" of being held by Aristotle. Epistemology and the understanding of the learning world-systems was opposite in these planes of Greek thought that was later on inherited by the Occident and by the atomistic and rationalist philosophers of Islamic scholasticism.

4.2   Relational Epistemology

Contrary to the idea of epistemology and ontology as metaphysical concepts, there are the more recent works on relational epistemology (Thayer-Bacon, 2003). Relational epistemology has to do with the "unity" of the universes and their entities through evolutionary learning. We have explained such phenomena by means of the relations of unification of knowledge arising from the foundations of the divine law and moral guidance.

In present times, relational epistemology has acquired deep interests among scientists and social philosophers in the subject of learning systems and complementarities between their entities. On the relational epistemology of social relations, Thayer-Bacon (p. 251) writes:

> A relational (e)pistemology argues that the relationships we experience with others are both personal and social: They are what Dewey called transactional relationships. We are first of all social beings who are greatly affected by others, but we also greatly affect others with our individual influence, right from the start.

On the theme of scientific relational epistemology, Thayer-Bacon (p. 264) continues:

> We learned from these scientists that the universe is a complicated, complementary web of relations that must be understood as an undivided whole, rather than analyzed into parts.

The project of unity of knowledge is epistemological along lines of relational epistemology, but with the substantive and revolutionary difference that the claimed "unity" of knowledge between the parts by relationalism is not a possibility of rationalism. In economics, the ideas of methodological individualism and Darwinian mutations by competition and substitution instead of premising on universally complementary relations, distort the relational understanding of organisms. Our arguments in earlier chapters have established that a functional and analytical way of interrelating, explaining and configuring the world-systems under unity of knowledge requires ultimate reduction of all questions and issues to the divine law, thereby seeking divine guidance on these matters.

4.2.1   *Referencing the example of neuro-cybernetics in E-O-O-E model*

An example here is the project of neuro-cybernetics taken in functional forms premised on the E-O-O-E configuration of the socio-scientific order. The E-O-O-E model was explained earlier. The axiom of circular cause and effect in this methodological order of unity of divine knowledge was explained by the topology of completeness of the divine law. This is a problem of establishing truth by taking recourse to the self-referencing arguments proving truth by its own reflexivity.

But what is a true or reasonable assumption? Our foregoing arguments point out that the limiting irreducible axiom of unity of divine
knowledge in *Tawhid* cannot be premised on human reason as the
primordial. Rather, human reason is a created entity on the basis of
Tawhid. Thus, our arguments in the previous chapter led us to crit-
ically establish the nature and credibility of the Tawhidi irreducible
premise on the basis of the divine law of unity of knowledge. The
understanding and interpretation of secondary rules and guidance
derived from the primal laws are subsequently discoursed in society.
This stage of development requires the function of reason.

In this way, a complementary invocation of revelation and reason
is used to derive a rule for socio-scientific investigation. In this regard,
the Qur'an declares (87: 1–3):

> Glorify the name of thy Guardian-Lord Most High, Who has created
> and further, given order and proportion; Who has ordained laws and
> granted guidance.

This entire provision of Qur'anic knowledge from the primordial
foundations to guidance, explanation, logical formulation and verification establishes the phenomenology pertaining to the E-O-O-E
worldview methodology. Conditions of consistency, coherence, predictability, explanation and verification of both complex phenomena as well as simple ones and premises of truth and falsehood are
all encapsulated within the irreducible axiom of Tawhidi unity of
knowledge.

Thus, if these criteria are not satisfied, then the alleged truth cannot be reasonable. Still less can it be reasonable if no serious attempt
is made to match the alleged truth against the criteria of observation,
formalism, inference and verification. Yet, the nature of many of the
concepts will differ from how they are oppositely derived in terms of
rational epistemology and the so-called revelation-reason complementary relations.

Briefly pointing out some such differences in the understanding of concepts are the meanings of equilibrium, simulation and
learning as coherent and consistent terms of the E-O-O-E worldview methodology. The combination of these characteristics in

the relational epistemological model of learning leads to the characterization of evolutionary equilibrium instead of steady-state ones, and the replacement of optimization calculus by simulation calculus (Choudhury and Korvin, 2002). Besides, predictability and sustainability of the E-O-O-E worldview methodology was argued to be prevalent over the largest domain of world-systems with their diverse and specific problems and issues.

In Chapter 3, we explained the universal nature of the Tawhidi unity of knowledge-centered worldview toward establishing this framework of the Universal Paradigm. Contrary to received socio-scientific doctrines and the philosophy of science that premises concepts, understanding, application and inferences on different theories of the disciplines, the Universal Paradigm overcomes such methodological differences. The methodology underlying all diverse issues remains unique. There are simply varieties of issues and problems for diverse cases. It is important to note how Myrdal (1977, p. 106) characterized such a unified approach to understanding and analysis. He stated:

> I came to see that in reality there are no economic, sociological, psychological problems, but just problems and they are all mixed and composite . . . .

4.3   Scientific Reductionism

Relational epistemology premised on unity of knowledge in its evolutionary learning space-time continuum denies the problem of reductionism beyond the point of the ultimate unity of the divine law and the world-systems so constructed. Contrary to reductionism, the irreducibility property of the Tawhidi worldview methodology is a search for and establishment of the foundational core of knowledge. It is both deductively and inductively derived by circular causation and is analytically established by proof. It adopts the theorem of self-referencing to prove truth by itself; falsehood by itself (Choudhury, 2002). The learning world-systems are thereby incomplete in knowledge. Therefore, in the open super-cardinal space of the E-O-O-E worldview, reductionism cannot prevail.

Reductionism leads to a partial study of problems that otherwise are interconnected and extended. Mainstream socio-scientific disciplines are thus found to be riddled with independently constructed compartments of disciplinary specialization. They sever interrelationship between them in the absence of a common epistemological praxis.

However, the point must be understood. We are not denying the need for specialization in specific problem-solving situations by disciplines. Rather, the methodological problematique arises by differentiation and alienation between different disciplines, issues and problems. Instead of such a characterization of the disciplines, the epistemology of unity of knowledge bestows a unique and universal worldview methodology that is commonly invoked in all disciplines for addressing diverse problems. The diversity of the disciplines is retained in respect of their issues and problems, despite the uniqueness of the epistemic methodology of unity of knowledge. Such a methodology was formalized by TSR.

4.4   The Neoclassical Economic Reductionism

Neoclassical economics claims full information on choices; economic decisions are thereby rational decisions; and methodological individualism resulting in competition replaces cooperation completely. The most starkly contradictory of such assumptions that stand out as nicety for problem-solving is found in neoclassical economic theory. This is the axiom of marginal rate of substitution — that two or more variables cannot coexist altogether. Scarcity of resources and economic competition lead them into conflict, and thereby, into tradeoffs, even though two of three of such substitutes may bundle together to marginalize the third one.

4.5   Introducing the Principle of Pervasive Complementarities Contra Neoclassical Axiom of Marginal Rate of Substitution

Contrary to this neoclassical axiom of marginal substitution is the natural principle of pervasive complementarities in the worldview methodology of unity of knowledge. It proves that in the face of knowledge flows premised on unity, the capacity to learn and co-evolve according to this precept increases. Participatory organization of life and thought emerges; and the assumption of scarcity and competition are replaced by abundance and shared opportunities. These conditions are the result of complementarities and their sustainability between state and polity variables. These together chart the path of evolutionary learning according to the episteme of unity of knowledge.

Certain social issues can be reflected upon in terms of the opposing praxis of unity of knowledge and neoclassicism. A lack of empathy and an inability to go beyond the narrow confines it has set for itself are two of the reasons why neoclassical economics cannot tackle the social problem of poverty alleviation. In other words, there is no robust theory of the formation, ownership and just distribution of wealth and resources in all of mainstream economics, particularly so in neoclassical economics. To answer these concerns, the entire precept of competition and scarcity must be replaced by the principle of cooperation, and thereby, of complementarities and participation.

Typically, conventional neoclassical economics believes in what is called the opportunity cost. That is, if somebody gains something, somebody else loses the equivalent. In this respect, the trade-off between economic interests and social goals leaves the latter at a disadvantage. Thus, conventional economics believes that no overall improvement in economics is possible and any improvement for the poor must inevitably involve a detriment for the rich, and vice versa.

4.6   Contrasting Worldviews of the Principle of Pervasive Complementarities and Marginalism

The following is a contrast between the principle of pervasive complementarities in the Universal Paradigm worldview methodology and marginal substitution (tradeoff) in neoclassical economics. Consider the case of Comparative Advantage doctrine in International Free Trade theory. National choices under this doctrine assume the prevalence of scarcity of resources and thus, make the argument that not everything can be simultaneously produced by every country for the purpose of specialization. The fact of the matter is, though, that there can be sufficient degree of production diversification and pooling of financial and physical resources and endowments to enhance the possibility to produce a diversity of final goods and services. Consequently, the agricultural producers and manufacturing producers would now cooperate to enlarge the output possibilities and recycle the same into resources to produce even more of such diversity.

This kind of dynamic advantage principle requires codetermination between state and institutional variables, rules, technological development and resource-sharing, and guidance for organizing the intersectoral linkages and pooling of shared resources and enterprise. Thereby, the enjoyment of proportionate production and profitability benefits are also shared. In the Edgeworth-Bowley resource allocation box in microeconomics, the contract points of mutual benefits between goods (Henderson and Quandt, 1971), and thereby agents underlying such producers and consumers, would perpetually shift the production possibility and the consumer indifference curves. This makes it impossible for any of such surfaces to remain stable, steady and well-defined to read relative prices, and therefore marginal rates of substitution. Consequently, neither the neoclassical opportunity cost nor its comparative advantage doctrine would apply.

The relative allocation of resources along an evolutionary learning trajectory of resource allocation will still apply, for this is formulated as contract under market-polity interaction (structural institutional discourse). But such points are neither steady-state equilibriums nor output optimization points in the case of the Universal Paradigm worldview methodology. They are points that can at best be approximated, but not fully attained in the Quantum Probability sense. Such evolutionary learning points belong to the field of possibilities for unity of knowledge.

The Universal Paradigm worldview methodology improves upon such analytical constrictions by making them meaningful, extensive and rigorous. New areas of analytical capacity, scientific reasoning and mathematical profundity are opened up by the Universal Paradigm. Thus, the arts of analyzing, classifying, predicting, assessing — but without the neglect of imagination, intuition and, in particular, social empathy — are ingrained in the Universal Paradigm with a critical investigation of the methods of reductionism in mainstream interdisciplinary fields.

Lastly, perhaps the greatest danger arising from reductionism is that, when the concept of overall systemic relationship between social entities is denied, moral concepts are in practice being weakened, even destroyed. That is bad enough in itself. But the weakening of morality disastrously combines with the weakening of empathy and the lack of relationship between parts to block the realization of, and the need for, paradigm shift. Such a debilitating combination prevents any understanding of the need for, and possibility of, overall socio-scientific change.

Indeed, the combination of a weakened morality, a weakened empathy and a failure to see circular causal interrelations between interdependent parts explains why neoclassical economics has no definitive concept of social change in respect of the good things of life. The very fact that neoclassical methodology accommodates the substitution between good (e.g., price stability) and bad (e.g., unemployment), as in the Phillip's Curve, shows that it promotes tradeoffs that are not only meaningless analytically, but also grossly unsocial in nature. Beyond economics, proponents of neoclassicism consider its methodology of competition, conflict, substitution and economic to be universal (Fukuyama, 1992).

4.7   New Epistemological Thinking in Human Ecology

Thankfully, fundamental epistemological questions are invading the intellectual scene and social activism today. There is an increasing realization for a need to outgrow the confines of a normal science into complex embedded system perspectives called symbiosis.

The modern human ecology movement is a good example for seeing the relevant system interconnections and then saying what needs to be, and can be, done. Indeed, it is to the eternal credit of environmental activists that, over recent decades, they have been able to draw links between phenomena and subjects to create a new paradigmatic understanding. This is the field of human ecology (Hawley, 1986). Without this challenging paradigm, the world would be largely unaware of the concepts of sustainable development and sustainability, which neoclassical economics in particular, and mainstream economics in general, cannot answer.

Chapter

5

Islamic Economics and Finance: The Moral Basis

Egotistical self-interest has not always been the case with human nature. The theme of global ethics is a case in point. Global ethics is the search for a universal paradigm of coexistence. Yet, the differentiation between ways of thinking on ethics is important to note. Ethics is of a humanistic nature. On the other hand, the derivation of ethics from the primacy of the moral law, and hence from the divine law, is a central issue in the social reconstruction of useful knowledge *vis-à-vis* the world-systems.

Inquiry in the direction of establishing the moral foundation of ethics and social order is essentially the groundwork of the epistemology of the Universal Paradigm worldview. In the E-O-O-E model, this foundation is shown by invoking and continuously "recalling" the injunction of the moral law through human-regimented discourse to discover rules and guidance according to the moral foundations. The moral foundations must thus be such as to be uniquely acceptable to reason. Yes, it may not necessarily be always acceptable to all people. The conflict between revelation and reason and ego thus darkens human perception to oppose reason for the sake of prejudice.

5.1   The Moral Law, Ethics and Human Experience

A formal causality between the moral law, the derivation of universal ethics there from, and the relevance of such a relationship with matters of diverse world-systems can be derived in reference to the epistemological worldview methodology of E-O-O-E. We proceed along these lines now.

Let

$$M(\theta^*, \mathbf{X}^*(\theta^*); \wp) \tag{5.1}$$

denote the analytical representation of the domain of moral law.

M denotes the representation of the moral law associated with the moral text. Such a moral text must be governed by the minimal number of axioms that can be universally accepted by all through the force of the text and reason, signifying complementarities between revelation and reason. The Qur'anic references in this regard are termed as *Ayaths* (verses). *Ayaths* are combined with the guidance of the Prophet Muhammad, known as the Sunnah. In reference to the universal propositional statements that we laid down in the Introduction to this work, such an *Ayath* is denoted by P_n; n denotes numbered reference to diverse and specific references to issues, directly or indirectly inferred with extensions in understanding.

Let θ^* belong to Ω, the divine premise of unity of knowledge as explicated in the most reduced and irreducible precept of Oneness of God and its meaning in the world-systems, self and the other. Such meanings are derived from a function of attributes that enable understanding of self and the other, and thereby, of the issues and problems of world-systems as they are and ought to be. The attributes are based on the deepening of belief in divine oneness. This experience enables two kinds of insights toward gaining understanding by the combination of belief and reason (revelation complementary with reason). It is a way of communion between the inner self resting on belief and reason with the inherent submission of the entities of world-systems to the divine law.

$\mathbf{X}^*(\theta^*)$ denotes mention in the Qur'an of the issues under investigation either directly referred to or inferred. Such normative references are ideal types. On the basis of these, the construction of the world-systems and specific issues are to be pursued in the real-world case.

℘ denotes the attribute function that carries the attributes of consciousness through reason into assertion. Otherwise, ℘ can be referred to as preference bundle formed by attributes of consciousness, belief and reason in response to reflections in the world-systems by reference to the Qur'an and by contemplation on the Signs of God (*Ayath Allah*). At the level of consciousness, ℘ denotes the unique and universal way among human beings toward comprehending the Oneness of God, and thus the unity of divine knowledge in the scheme of all things. ℘ thereby underlies the cause and effect of *Tasbih* (intrinsic worship) and *Fitra* (divine essence for goodness), as these terms were explained earlier.

5.1.1   *An example of the moral law and its cognition*

We take the example of the Qur'anic description of markets as an edict of the moral law on this specific issue. The ideal description of market process is done in terms of the Qur'anic *Ayaths* (verses) relating to markets within the grand ecology and values in extant. The normative Qur'anic model of markets is consciously understood by the passage of deepening self-consciousness of the Signs of Oneness of God in the scheme of "everything".

In the case of market process, the moral law and the combination of belief and reason establishes the grand ecological nature of market systems. These are revealed in the text of the Qur'an and the Sunnah. The references also point out the grand ecological well-being effects of the attenuating market concept. The grand ecological order explained by the *Ayaths* (Signs of God) reflects unity of the divine law as the intrinsic character of mind-matter consciousness. The concept of ecology is now derived from the description of a unified and worshipping world-system in terms of specific issues, problems and their extensions by discursive learning. This is the idea of sustainability.

The common core of communion between self and other, as in ecological balance, and as identified in the Qur'anic *Ayaths*, conveys the meaning of Islamic worship. It exists as consciousness expressed by the submission of mind and matter to the precept of Oneness of God as the core of the divine law. Such mind-matter communion is realized in terms of consciousness of the unity of knowledge as the Oneness of God presented in the intrinsic property of "everything". It is referred to as *Tasbih*.

Tasbih is thereby active worshipping in response to the conscious recognition of divine unity as the core of the moral law. On the other hand, the nature of oneness that is the intrinsic essence in the mind and matter of "everything" is known as *Fitra*. *Tasbih* and *Fitra* are inherent in mind and matter. The search for *Tasbih* in mind-matter experience comes through practical ways of worshipping God for asserting God's attribute of oneness in living experience. Active worship is referred to as *Ibadah*.

5.1.2   *A formalism in respect of the moral law and ethics*

Let $\langle \{\theta^*, \mathbf{X}(\theta^*); \wp\} \rangle$ denote the outer cover of the divine law expressed as consciousness according to the total concept of the super-cardinal topology of the divine origin and end denoted by Ω. Since the Qur'an says that the revealed Qur'an has its origin in the Mother of the Book (*Lauh Mahfuz*), therefore the Qur'an claims its details in "everything" to be in perfected extant. But the Mother of the Book comprises the ultimate completion of knowledge. The attribute of completion of knowledge and its representation here as an open ($\langle . \rangle$) super-cardinal topological space is denoted by $\langle \{\theta^*, \mathbf{X}(\theta^*); \wp\} \rangle \subseteq \Omega$. The function of $\langle . \rangle$ is to span the domain of consciousness generated by combining *Tasbih*, reason and cognition by all possible topologies of $\{\theta^*, \mathbf{X}(\theta^*); \wp\}$.

In reference to our example of Qur'anic meaning of markets, the market precepts are understood at the level of consciousness. In methodological formalism, this stage is not still the stage of ontological existentialism that is followed by ontic applications and inferences. Market is conceptualized normatively by the Qur'anic *Ayaths* (verses) on markets, ecology, systems and well-being, together with their extensions, as reason perceives these attributes through human understanding capacitated by *Tasbih*, combined with reflective observations. The latter are called by the *Ayaths* as Signs of the Oneness of God.

The role of $\theta^* \in \Omega$ in formulating the moral law can now be noted:

$$\Omega \supseteq \langle \{\theta^*, \mathbf{X}(\theta^*); \wp\} \rangle \qquad (5.2)$$

= Qur'anic text spanning all knowledge in everything with its completion in Ω as the super-cardinal complete, outer cover (Halmos, 1974) $\equiv \Omega$ as the fullness of the divine law.

$\rightarrow$ (Qur'anic *Tasbih*, *Ayaths* transmitted by Sunnah) Moral Law $\equiv M\{\theta^*, \mathbf{X}(\theta^*); \wp\}$

$\rightarrow$ (transmission of the Moral Law to world-systems through discourse) = $\{\theta, \mathbf{X}(\theta);$ preferences formed by IIE-processes through discourse$\}$

$\rightarrow$ Rest of the E-O-O-E processes in space-time continuums $\equiv$ domain of deriving the Islamic Law (the Shari'ah)

Thus, the Shari'ah is a part of the phenomenological construction and explanation of the world-systems that are patterned on the basis of the Moral Law as derived from the Qur'an and the Sunnah. While the primal domain, $\Omega \supseteq \langle\{\theta^*, \mathbf{X}(\theta^*); \wp\}\rangle$ is premised purely on the episteme of Oneness of God (unity of the divine law), so also are the Moral Law and the Shari'ah. Inculcating the attributes for knowing divine oneness, understanding in depth the *Ayaths* (verses) and externalizing these to the unified world-systems form the ultimate axiom of the Qur'anic worldview. These together characterize the worldview methodology of the Universal Paradigm.

Now the recalling of (Ω, S) in the E-O-O-E phenomenology along the space-time continuums spanned by $\Omega \supseteq \langle\{\theta^*, \mathbf{X}(\theta^*); \wp\}\rangle$, gives the ultimate and unique source of the knowledge-centered world-systems of unity of divine knowledge as explained by the Tawhidi worldview.

5.1.3   *Ethics and the moral law*

The origin of the knowledge-centered world-systems of unity of knowledge being $\Omega \supseteq \langle\{\theta^*, \mathbf{X}(\theta^*); \wp\}\rangle$, therefore, the moral law is the ultimate source of ethics. Besides, the reasoned uniqueness and universality of the praxis of moral law so explained causes the nature of ethics premised on the moral law to be universal in nature. Thus, we come to the regime of global ethics in the sense of its uniqueness and universality as determined by the moral law.

In this sense and interpretation, we now define Global Ethics, $E(.)$, as follows: $E(\langle\{\theta, \mathbf{X}(\theta);$ preferences formed by IIE-processes through discourse = $\wp_{ij...}$ preferences formed by IIE-processes through discourse between ij ... systems, agents, variables etc. $\}\,\rangle$).

Note that in the definition of $E(\langle\,.\,\rangle)$, if its primordial premise in the moral law is left out, the definition will still hold in the procedural sense, but will fail to have a substantive meaning. The consequences of this analytical difference are great, for, in the procedural case, we return to the rationalist design of knowledge formation. We would then understand a learning world-system under the impact of muta-tions or disequilibrium dynamics. Unity of knowledge is impossible in such mutative systems.

Markets as an ecological sub-system modelled in reference to the Qur'anic meaning of ethical behavior must derive their ethics of exchange, resource allocation and appropriateness of goods and ser-vices on the basis of $E(\langle\,.\,\rangle)$, which is derived from the moral law.

If the characterization of market process follows the $E(\langle\,.\,\rangle)$-dynamics other than the moral law as given above, the episteme of unity of knowledge is abandoned. Thereby, the principle of pervasive complementarities between Shari'ah compliant possibilities does not abide. Now, neoclassical economic properties of marginal substitu-tion tradeoffs take over. Scarcity of resources, conflict and competi-tion militate against participatory mechanisms of resource generation, sharing and mobilization. The nature of goods, social contracts, insti-tutional rules and policies are all turned in the direction of supporting the neoclassical transformation. In the end, the relational character of world-systems as seen in terms of interlocking unity of knowledge at the core, despite having diversity of problems and issues, disappears.

5.1.4   *The example of financial interest (Riba) in the order of moral and ethical laws*

A central ethical concern in relation to the moral and ethical law and world-systems is that of interest. We ask, what is the rate of interest? How is it related to the socioeconomic relations? How has it been treated in history?

It is true that the imposition of interest has been viewed by major religions as a social malaise. Aristotle (Barker, 1999) abhorred the craving for wealth but considered interest as a necessary evil. Thomas Aquinas (Blaug, 1968) treated usury as social evil, but accepted the market rate of interest. Indeed, to protect society's integrity and means of self-support for its members, every religion in history perceived that the system of usury — in particular, rural usury — was opposed to the proper workings of society.

Sauer (2002, pp. 97–118, edited) provides good details of the history of financial interest in Judeo-Christian religious tradition and compares it to the Islamic case. He writes:

> Both traditions agree what acts constitute an interest transaction is viz. a description of the acts involved. However, there is substantial disagreement about what is exchanged in an interest-bearing transaction and, so, its meaning.

> Islamic financial institutions regard all forms of interest as immoral and so illicit. "Christian" financial institutions regard most interest-bearing transactions as moral and so only some kinds of interest-bearing transactions as illicit. The origin of these differences is metaphysical as well as ethical (p. 97).

Sauer goes on to say (p. 99):

> Islamic metaphysics are integrally interactive rather than substantive. This means that understanding of the world focuses on the relations of things rather than their nature or essence. It is processive rather than static. What a thing is, is framed by its relationships in processes, not its essence or necessary structure. This metaphysics is based on the view that creation is the locus of God's revelation as law and word governs the created order, and human activity must be ordered to the universe, i.e., to divine reality and order.

Contrary to the stern Islamic ruling on interest and the economic transaction, Sauer points out that the Christian practice of the law of interest was shaped primarily in the scholastic period. It was argued that as long as the delivery of the good and service was in accordance with their market values, the price of goods was socially acceptable. Thereby, concepts such as jus pretium *vis-à-vis* jus divinum were promoted to denote the sum of wage, cost of materials and a gain. Consequently, neither the precision nor the measurement of a moderate gain was objectively established. In this sense, the scholastic theory of interest, money and prices remained a variant of the latter days' theory of interest as a subjective time-preference measure.

In conclusion, it is found that avoidance of interest remained a moral law embedded in the Qur'an, the Sunnah and the Shari'ah in Islam. Thereby, the ethical law of interest, money and price was linked with the divine law in relation to market transactions embedded in human ecological domain. Thus, the ethical law relating to interest abolition is derived from the moral law in Islam. In other religious practices, interest rested in a sociocultural tradition that defined the ethical meaning. With the process of time, this conception of what is objective in the human formulation of the ethical law differed. Subsequently, the ethical law departed from the moral law.

In this regard, Sauer (p. 116) points out:

> Aquinas argued that it is morally licit to borrow at interest provided the borrower has a "good (i.e., licit, morally justifiable) end" in view, such as the relief of one's own or another's need. John Calvin, who marks the earliest Christian break with scholastic doctrine on interest, pursues this argument at length as reason to limit but not to prohibit the practice.

5.2 Interest and Usury

The Qur'an refers to interest and usury equivalently as *Riba* in terms of its evil effects on the equal, just and productive distribution of resources. This *Riba* rule applies to excesses in both financial contracts (*Riba al-Fadl*) and fungibles (*Riba al-Nasia*). It also applies to all forms of interest — nominal, real, effective, simple and compound.

In regards to the general definition of *Riba* relating to all forms and measures of gifts and exchanges, the Qur'an (Chapter 30, verse 39) says:

> And that which you give in gift in order that it may increase your wealth from other's property, has no increase with Allah; but that which you give in charity seeking Allah's Countenance, then those they shall have manifold increase.

Regarding the unacceptability of all forms of interest, we can infer from the following Qur'anic verse by using the idea of the term of structure of interest rates. The Qur'an says (3:130):

> O you who believe! Devour not Riba, doubled and multiplied; but fear Allah; that you may prosper.

Now it is well-known from the theory of the term structure of interest rates that any simple (i.e., one-period) interest rate can be expressed as the compound of interest rates over many smaller time periods or contingencies within a given time horizon. Besides, because nominal rates are abolished in the *Riba* rule, therefore, real rates cannot exist: the real rate is the nominal rate net of the rate of change in price level (inflation rate). Nominal rate is abolished by the financial and real economic interrelationship, which also, by means of the direct productivity consequences of such an interrelationship, causes the rate of increase in money to equal the rate of increase in real economic returns. Consequently, inflationary conditions caused by a mismatch of the above-mentioned two rates cannot exist. The equations of nominal versus real with inflation rates are therefore unacceptable in Islamic economic relations. What does away the anomaly respecting all forms of interest rates and the rate of inflation are both the complementary relationship between money and real economy in the absence of interest rates, and the institutional and policy actions necessary to realize such complementarities.

Regarding the Qur'anic principle of just measure in gifts and exchanges, there is this verse (2:279):

> And if you do not do it (i.e., give up Riba), then take a notice of war from Allah and His Messenger, but if you repent, you shall have your *capital sums*. Deal not unjustly and you shall not be dealt with unjustly.

The Qur'an strongly forbids *Riba* on grounds of its inhuman nature to acquire for self at the expense of social justice, equitable distribution of wealth and well-being for others. Instead, the Qur'an points out that the latter attributes a rise through the medium of solidarity, cooperation and productive activity in the good things of life.

Imam Shatibi explains the conception of such good things of life as the combination of necessaries (*Dhururiyath*), comforts (*Hajiyath*) and refinements (*Tahsaniyath*), all of which belong to the hierarchy of dynamic life-fulfilling goods and services.

Several verses testify to this interconnection between the abolition of *Riba* and the institutions of trade, charity and social well-being. On the matter of causality between charity, trade, prosperity and social well-being, the Qur'an (2:274–275) declares:

> Those who (in charity) spend of their goods by night and day, in secret and in public, have their reward with their Lord: On them shall be no fear, nor shall they grieve. Those who devour Riba will not stand except as stands one whom the Evil One by his touch has driven to madness. That is because they say: "Trade is like Riba". But Allah has permitted trade and forbidden Riba .....

On the matter of causality between spending in the good things of life and attainment of social well-being thereby, is the verse (2:265):

> And the likeness of those who spend their substance, seeking to please Allah and to strengthen their souls, is as a garden, high and fertile: heavy rain falls on it but makes it yield a double increase of harvest, and if it receives not heavy rain, light moisture suffices it. Allah sees well whatever you do.

The interrelationships between the abolition of *Riba* rule, social productivity and well-being attained through trade and charity are important to note. There are causal relations between the abolition of *Riba* and the implementation of the cooperative and participatory financial instruments of resource mobilization, such as profit-sharing, equity participation and trade. These generate and mobilize productive spending in the good things of life and bring about participation at all ranks of society, thereby causing entitlement and empowerment.

On the injunction regarding the good things of life in production, consumption, exchange and distribution, the Qur'an (2:267) declares:

> O you who believe! Give of the good things which you have (honourably) earned, and of the fruits of the earth which you have produced for you, and do not even aim at getting anything which is

bad, in order that out of it you may give away something, when you yourself would not receive it except with closed eyes. And know that Allah is Free of all wants, and worthy of all praise.

5.3   A General Equilibrium Perspective of Interrelationships between Resource Expansion and Phasing Out of Interest Rates

The evolving circular causation interrelationships mentioned above are too detailed to be elaborated here. Yet, the salient features need to be stated.

Consider Phase One of a circular causation process as the following relation: Abolition of *Riba* causes mobilization of financial resources through its linkage with real resource development. This causes employment, profitability, equity and efficiency, entitlement, empowerment and social security to emerge as elements of the total social well-being.

Phase One then connects with a reverse Phase Two: Acquired levels of productivity gain, attained social well-being and resource mobilization in the midst, cause renewed confidence on the abolition of *Riba* rule, which is then reinforced both by economic and social relations and policies.

Yet another Phase Three can be the following — from the side of acquired social well-being to enhanced policy on real and financial resource linkage, and thereby, toward the regeneration of Phases One and Two.

Many such phases of circular causation interrelationships and transformations can be determined. Such a circular causality implies systemic learning gained by grand complementarities between variables and policies. These combine markets, economic, social, ethical and institutional factors and the underlying human preferences that influence the socioeconomic organization of life and thought relating to the abolition of *Riba*.

Such interaction between variables across phases of systemic learning by complementarities as explained above are centrally premised on three fundamental properties. They are naturally embodied in the Qur'anic outlook on learning systems. The properties are namely, interaction (reflected in the Qur'anic principle of diversity, **I**), integration or complementarities (reflected in the Qur'anic principle of the paired universes, **I**), both of these leading to creative evolution (**E**). Creative evolution and continuity of the same three phases of learning (**IIE**) is derived from the Qur'anic principle of reorigination, i.e., of knowledge flows in Qur'anic world-systems, the *Alameen*.

The IIE-process so established becomes pervasively knowledge-induced *ad infinitum* and across life's diverse issues. Such a circular causation by complementarities between the real and financial (monetary) resources causing attainment of social well-being (a comprehensive meaning of charity) is the central principle underlying the abolition of *Riba* or Usury rule of the Qur'an.

5.4 Interest and Usury in Social Models

The imposition of interest is a major cause of inequity, inequality, and loss of entitlement, empowerment and accountability. All of these combine with each other to militate against poverty alleviation. But in the Islamic sense of *Riba*, an undue increase is more than simply an unproductive and undue financial surplus. *Riba* also includes undue excess in material exchange contracts, or an increase in price and profits as surpluses and profiteering.

Riba being a socioeconomic variable entering exchange contract, is viewed both from the buyer's and the seller's sides of the contract. A consumer sees *Riba* as a hurtful charge on his potential income. *Riba* limits the potential of consumer spending in the good things of life. It thereby decreases consumer well-being that would be potentially derived from the acquirement of such goods and services. In the Islamic case, the potential augmentation of well-being from the provision of goods and services must also be tied to their Shari'ah compatibility.

From the producer's (seller's) viewpoint, including businesses of all sizes, productive allocation of the financial and other forms of resources increases the potential mobilization of such resources. The absence of interest on the side of input purchases, and thereby, the absence of interest on the payments to such productive factors, realizes potential resource mobilization, now to the benefit of both the consumer and the producer. This is a general equilibrium result that reflects the simulated position of social well-being for the consumer and the producer simultaneously.

Yet, the scenario of general equilibrium here is not of the neo-classical type. Non-existence of a neoclassical general equilibrium in exchange between buyers and sellers is due to the principle of pervasive complementarities that prevails on both sides of the exchange.

The well-being function of the consumer is characterized now to measure the degree of complementarities gained through IIE-process between the state and institutional variables in any given phase of learning on the premise of systemic unity of knowledge.

On the side of the producer, the production function is defined by complementary relations between the productive factors. The production contract between productive factors too is the result of polity and market interrelationships.

In the Tawhidi worldview methodology, such interrelations are explained by the circular causations between the entities characterizing the state and institutional variables in the presence of knowledge flows premised on unity of knowledge. At the end, the conditions of scarcity of resources, and thereby of optimality and full information, are rejected. Consequently, the simulated points of general ethico-economic equilibrium in exchange are points of evolutionary learning. As mentioned earlier, such geometrical points can be determined in the probabilistic sense only in a neighborhood of "cover" around the evolutionary equilibrium points, not absolutely.

5.5   Introducing Poverty in the *Riba* Relation

In view of the inequitable nature of interest rates, consider the example interrelating interest rate to poverty. We examine this issue first from the individual consumer's point of view, then from the viewpoint of the producer (business).

In the economy, there are rich and poor individuals who need funds for investment. In conventional theory, these funds come from past savings of the rich. The rich save following incentives that they acquire from interest. Thus, their expectation is for a higher rate of interest to undertake higher levels of savings. Contrarily, if interest rates remained low, the rich would switch funds between stocks, shares and bonds. If the interest rate was zero, all resources would be driven into productive investments comprising stocks and shares. Bonds and savings will not exist. Saving is thus contrary to resource mobilization.

Take an example. Let a rich person save $100,000 at an interest rate of 10%. Thereby, saving is encouraged, say for one time period. The total interest return on savings after one time period equals $10,000. Furthermore, say that the total income (including wealth of the rich saver) is $1 million at the beginning of the year. The percentage of his saving to income equals 10%. The rich person's income after one year equals $1,010,000.

In the same way, let the poor marginal saver save, say, 5% of his income of $10,000 (i.e., $500) to earn $500 at the end of the year in interest income. The poor man's year-end income equals $10,500.

Total output at the end of a year = $1,020,500.

Now, under the prevailing interest regime, the percentage of total wealth gap caused by interest between the rich and poor = approx. 100%.

The empowerment gap between the poor and rich in terms of savings = (10,000 − 500)/10,000 = 95%.

Next, on viewing the problem from the business side, we note that the culture of business, markets and profitability projected by the saving culture calls for a loss in potential resource mobilization to growth and development. In the above example, a potential output of $(100,000 + 10,000) between the rich and poor would have been injected into the economy in businesses and projects of all sizes and durations. This would yield an investment return from the time this resource has been mobilized into investments of all different durations. An example of short-term investment is trade financing. Thus, the potential wealth of the economy increases without withdrawal through total spending in investments and consumption, government participation in shareholding (e.g., Amanah Saham unit trusts in Malaysia) and in mandatory charity (*Zakat*) for enabling participation at the grassroots.

So how do the above calculations appear under resource mobilization? At 10/12 expected monthly percent rate of return on spending (private and social), the income in the one-period participatory economy equals:

$(1 million + 10,000) = \$1,010,000 \times (1 + 0.10/12)^{12} = \$1,977,603$ as total output.

This figure is higher than the total output in the case of savings as withdrawal of $1,977,603 - \$1,020,500 = \$957,103$.

Thus, potential output is lost in an interest-bearing economy. The sub-potential output causes loss of participatory productive activities. The poor cannot get into the potential output to generate incomes by participatory means with the rich and with others in their group. On the side of businesses, the loss of participatory businesses cannot diversify the product and risk to generate expansion of productive capacity, cost reduction, technological diffusion and economic and social stability.

Participation between consumers and producers in a communal sense, which is a critical cause and effect of resource mobilization, is also the medium for empowerment and entitlement in socioeconomic development. The resultant consequences on equality and distributive equity, simultaneous realization of economic efficiency and distributive equity, are gained. The participatory process induces linkages by the use of knowledge-induced development financing instruments and structural change through the socioeconomic IIE-processes. The moral and ethical relevance of such choices, as spending in the good things of life, is thus invoked. This is the case with the E-O-O-E methodology.

5.6   Debt Financing Consequences of Interest on Poverty

Debt is caused in two ways. Firstly, unpaid amounts of financial obligation from previous times (deficits) exist due to a loss in potential income caused by financial withdrawal and overextension of spending beyond existing resource availability. Savings cause financial withdrawal (Ventelou, 2005). Secondly, overextension of spending causes abandonment of the needs economy and its replacement by a wants economy (Levine, 1988). The ethical relevance is lost and the moral implications of the ethics of a needs economy remain unrealized due to the absence of proper instruments in the prevailing bad regimes of growth, distribution and development caused by regimes of rising interest and savings. Contrarily, it is both impossible and contrary to the resource mobilization regimes of growth, distribution and development to hold debt.

In the above-mentioned example, debt is created in the case of an economy focused on savings by the loss of the potential output. This potential output loss amounts to $$957,103. A resultant borrowing is required to replace this lost potential output. This replacement comes from borrowing, which in turn causes deficits, and thereby, debt. On the other hand, in the moral and ethical contexts, there is no need to develop an economy at a time beyond the extended possibility caused by the potential amount $1,977,603.

By expanding aggregate demand beyond potential output, the otherwise moral and ethical responsibility to cut back on wants as opposed to needs is left out from the budgetary process. National income then shows skewed weighting in favor of wants as opposed to needs. Thereby, growth is focused on the well-being of the rich. Consequently, the national income increases with heightened economic growth, but at the expense of social goods and distributive equity. This is the perennial problem of efficiency-equity tradeoff of mainstream economics of growth and development.

In the above example, the sub-potential output, if generated in the economy by means of resource mobilization, would generate employment and sustainable development right from the moment of resource injection. No waiting time is needed. Contrarily, the savings hypothesis argues that in the course of time, the sub-potential withdrawal from national output can be reinjected as investment at that time. This is flawed reasoning. Firstly, savings as withdrawal from potential output remains a continuous economic consequence over the life of the economy. Hence, there is continuous withdrawal from potential output all along. Consequently, all along the economic life there is loss of potential social benefits, such as employment; sustainability by production diversity in dynamic regimes of needs, cost and risks-sharing; and gains in empowerment and entitlement by economy-wide and society-wide participation among all segments of society. Now, distributive equity as a goal complementary with economic efficiency is attainable and is measured by means of simulation of the well-being function. In this way, poverty alleviation is addressed.

5.7 Conclusion

Our first set of applications of the epistemology of unity of knowledge according to the implications of the general phenomenology expressed in the E-O-O-E methodology has stood up to the test. In reference to this praxis, this chapter showed that realization of unity of knowledge in diverse issues and problems of socio-scientific nature necessarily and sufficiently emanates from the moral law. The starting point of any such goal based on the ethical premise alone, without fundamentally arising from the moral roots of the divine law, is untenable. The vagaries of human rationalism contrary to the precise episteme of divine oneness and of the divine law take control and steer away reason from its essentially unified worldview.

Once the epistemological foundations of the law of unity of knowledge are established on the moral law, from which the idea of global ethics is drawn, then many of the human actions follow accordingly. In this regard, we have discussed the important issues of poverty alleviation and global justice in terms of abolition of interest and debt. These issues were taken up in a methodological way in reference to the working of the E-O-O-E model and the precincts of the moral law.

Chapter

6

Tawhidi Questions of Technology and Technological Change

6.1 On Technological Questions

Technology means appropriateness of the means of production and their utilization and adaptability in generating well-being for all beings. The natural inclination to explore the capabilities of nature and to use human endeavor to tap these goals for the security, comfort and essential needs triggered technological development of its own. Yet, today, as we examine the topic of technology and technological advancement, it is seen not to be an innocent and natural tendency in human societies. Rather, with the advance of self-centered ego of modern ways of looking at resources, competition and material acqui-sition, the meaning and implications of technology and technological change have also become power-centered.

In this chapter we will inquire into the meaning, nature and scope of technology from the opposite viewpoints of modern world-system and that of the episteme of unity of knowledge of the Universal Paradigm. We will then examine the implications of these two ways of understanding technology and technological change in respect of human well-being.

Our emphasis in this book being on unity of knowledge as the epistemic foundations of socio-scientific reasoning, we will evaluate the intellectual debate from this vantage point. We have established in Chapter 5 that the origins of unity of knowledge for human well-being is in the moral law, from which emanates the field of universal ethics. This premise will continue to ground our critical examination of the theme of technology and technological change.

6.2   A Social Context of Technology

Technology is ingrained on adaptation and social well-being. One of the ways of explaining this is by the choice of factors of production and adaptation to skills. In this regard, development economics is well-known to base distributional questions of well-being upon the output/factor ratios. However, in the neoclassical approach to development economics, such choices assume underlying marginal rates of substitution between the competing factors while maximizing output with scarce budget that is competed for by the factors of production. The possibility of defining complementarities between the factors in the development and production processes is rendered impossible. Technology thus becomes socially demeaning.

6.3   Technology and Technological Change According to E-O-O-E Methodology

Technology becomes a key medium for the transformation of the productive relations into cooperative forms and taking it away from the neoclassical form of competition, resource scarcity and its central postulate of marginal substitution. In this sense, the meaning of technology according to E-O-O-E model is that of ways and means that adapt a rule of unification between capital and labor and other artefacts for human well-being. The artefacts belong to a vast domain of production processes and choices in both intermediate goods and services, final goods and services and know-how. The technology now aims at establishing learning interlinkages between the factors, while diversifying production, costs and risks to other similar possibilities as well, as these emerge from the learning experience. Knowledge flows arising from the learned experiences of production linkages and discovery of new possibilities expand continually across production and cost diversifications. Thus, there come about unification and inductive effects between artefacts and their other coterminous premises, such as learning, resource-sharing, know-how, adaptability, social participation, and intersectoral, project-wide and agent-specific linkages.

Technological change is the result of the nature of technology embalmed in the above definition and meaning of technology. For example, the effectiveness of unification of knowledge and knowledge-induced entities in the midst of production diversifications and cost/risk-diversifications bring about well-being in terms of unification between all such possibilities. Technological change is then explained by the progressive simulation of the well-being criterion. It summarizes the entire program of unity of knowledge as a system phenomenon and the selection of appropriate goods, services, means and opportunities that appertain to the moral law followed by ethical implications.

It was explained earlier that the coterminous actions of market forces (state variables representing specific entities) and polity variables represented by the choice of institutional and policy instruments are denoted by specific vector of explanatory endogenous and learning variables of the well-being function. Simulation of this criterion under the condition of circular causation between the variables summarizes the evidential (ontic) phase, which then is followed by further evolutionary learning in continuum. This kind of learning dynamics signifies the development characteristics of technological change over domains of unity of knowledge between the knowledge-induced entities.

An example is given here to bring out the meaning and nature of technology and technological change. The questions we pose are subtle ones: Which is the appropriate social and efficient decision? Should the user be moved at the disposal of technology? Or, should technology be moved at the disposal of the user? Finally, is there a possibility to link up these two movements into circular causality that marks complementary factor and productive relations?

6.3.1   *Case 1: User moved towards technology*

This option is tantamount to asking the user to develop its productive capacity according to the demands of technology. Now, technology comes about by the pressure of market forces and the ability and competition of large program developers to supply such business demands. Since markets are run by the forces of competition and self-centered preferences and menus, thereby, the heightened technological demand of such a market system will put challenges on the user to rise up to the technological standards. Opportunities to do so need sophisticated educational systems and financial and other resource opportunities. These do not lie within the reach of marginalized sections of society. Consequently, technology and technological development become demeaning for the marginalized groups, while being elitist acquisitions for the powerful business world and privileged users and consumers of technological outputs.

The moral question of distributive equity along with productive efficiency is sacrificed. The mere ethical question in such a case would be to endow technology and its users with the socially determined privileges for power, authority and wealth in accordance with the private ownership question alone. Such a determination is not always in accordance with the moral question, though it can be an ethical one. John Locke dwelled on this issue of the moral limits of ownership in Western civilization.

In Islamic belief, the moral question abounds everywhere. Most significantly, it is found linked with the question of abolition of interest and its substitution by participatory development-financing instruments. These are principally the profit and loss sharing, trade financing and secondary financing instruments revolving around the primary ones. There is also the mandatory instrument of wealth taxation (*Zakat*) together with voluntary charity (*Sadaqah*). These now integrate with the total socially productive, development and distributional relations.

The meaning and scope of technology and technological change in modernist traditions are flawed perceptions of reality. Take the case of the relationship between science, technology and organization in reference to their ethical relevance. Choudhury (1993, p. 43) writes:

> If physical theories claim independence of their own, then they must be of the nature of methodological independence and individuation in the total field of science. Thereby, all the characteristics of peer support and interest groups must stand for these individuated scientific groups. Truth is then relative to these segmented fields. There is no necessary convergence to a unique premise of knowledge except to the random variations in limitless fields of evolutionary epistemologies.

The relationship between science, technology and organization is further extended to the economic field. Choudhury (*ibid.*, p. 45) continues (edited):

> Trained manpower is required by cause and effect to sustain this system or else it finds itself out of demand. Thus the same ethical question in regards to thought (science) and practice (organization) is invoked in occidental formula of human resource development in the midst of scientific theories of economics. The present days' malaise of industrial unemployment, structural industrial shifts in the direction of capital using ones; the accumulation of debts; and the displacement of traditional ways of survival by post-modernist attitudes toward sustainability as costly development of capital equipments, are some of the examples of the relations between labor, capital, human resources and organizational theory.

6.3.2   *Case 2: Technology moved towards user*

In this case, the design and evolution of technology adapts to the available skills of the user. The resulting kind of technological change is socially acceptable, but not necessarily dynamic in the economic and social sense. In other words, in the interest of social goals, it is possible in this case to lose the important supportive means of economic regeneration that can perpetuate on the basis of intertwined social transformation. The neoclassical model underlying technological change is no different from Case 1 given previously. The exception simply is that the resource allocation trajectory in technology is biased towards social goals causing tradeoff in the economic goals. This was the case with socialism. It collapsed both as a scientific and a practical model of technological and social change.

An example in this case is of environment sustainability as a technological goal of the social type. Sustainable development as so construed has lost universal appeal since it became a political agenda of the Rio Earth Summit. The concept of sustainable development has since been replaced by that of sustainability comprising the broader human ecological domain as its field of investigation. Yet, do we have a methodology to investigate this broader holistic conception of well-being in the existing socioeconomic theory and methodology?

Problems in the sustainable development conception and sustainability in the absence of an adept methodology to study its holistic nature arise from the continued treatment of the environment and ecology as a final good. In that sense, it is either a consumer good or a capital good according to economic analysis. Consequently, it is essential to consider these artefacts as being subject to depreciation. Scarcity of resource and its allocation are at the heart of the economic analysis that banks upon opportunity cost between environment and economic growth. Thereby, the inputs of production that generate the environmental production function or include environment in the economic growth model must treat input demand as derived demand. In this, the marginal rate of substitution (tradeoff) between environment and economic growth, productivity and efficiency, necessarily treat the inputs of production, capital, labor and environment as substitutes (postulate of marginalism).

The marginalist perception of environment-related tradeoffs would also influence the mindset of the decision-makers and organizations that promote particular forms of technology and technological change. The cost engendered by resource and factor substitutions is quite large, since the need for sustainability necessitates a vast number of linkages. These are ignored in neoclassical economic methodology. Instead, neoclassical economics is premised on competing and differentiated alternatives caused by tradeoff between them, when its objective is optimization of output in a production relation that treats the environment as a physical resource subject to scarcity caused by competition and differentiation between alternatives. These are sure signs of loss of learning and complementarities between the productive factors and social artefacts, and the economy and human ecology with environment in its midst.

6.3.3   *Case 3: Causality between technology and productive usage*

The epistemology of unity of knowledge, premised on the moral law from which the ethical meaning is derived, redefines technology and configures the scope of technological change differently. Thereby, a new social contract is simulated in relation to market forces and institutional restructuring, keeping in view the interrelationships between state variables and institutional variables (policy variables). The E-O-O-E model is invoked. Unity of knowledge now pertains to the Tawhidi (Oneness of God = unity of the divine law) methodology discussed earlier.

Technology comprises embedded ways and means of adapting the know-how and social and economic artefacts to produce learning linkages. To generate technological change, the evolutionary learning linkages establish causality in the presence of unification of knowledge between various entities (variables and agents) that learn along expanding systems of socio-scientific possibilities (see Choudhury, 2004, pp. 202–226).

Recycling of technologies is attained by creating layers of interconnecting technologies out of older ones. Thereby, substitution and replacement (except by a penultimate equipment retirement) in the technology domain are rejected to make room for complementarities and production and cost/risk-diversifications in the layers of technology (Azid, 2001; Mathur, 1977). The absence of tradeoffs and their replacement by extensive complementarities along evolutionary paths of learning in unity of knowledge redefines the interrelationships between technology, society, economy, institution and science.

A new concept of sustainability arises in view of such wider embedded fields of complementarities. Indeed, the principle of pervasive complementarities is a necessary and sufficient condition for gaining evidence of the unity of divine knowledge at work across systemic circular causation. Without this principle in place, the circular causation relations cannot be defined and estimated. The well-being function would then remain undefined.

6.3.4   *Combining case 1 and case 2 together with case 3*

Combining Case 1 and Case 2 together in Case 3 implies that learning in evolutionary paths of linkages as the sign of unification of knowledge between know-how, entities and sustainability between these requires circular causation to exist between the variables and entities of the two sides feeding into each other by way of sustaining both. An example we take up here to explain the complementary conception of technology, technological change and the sustainability precept in the light of unity of knowledge is with respect to appropriate technology. A sustainable biodiversity regime is maintained both across entities and technological change.

Choudhury (1993, p. 68) explains in this way: we consider appropriate technology as the one that generates dynamic basic-needs regimes of development. A country commences its development process by enabling users to adapt to the available technology. Hence, Case 2 is pursued. The social and ethical implications of this case are implied. But even as Case 2 gets implemented along the dynamic basic-needs regimes of development, simultaneously the adopted technology is endogenously developed to higher levels of know-how and circular causation. Now Case 1 is implied and the user is evolved endogenously in connection with its adaptation with the technology in Case 2. The ensuing production and cost/risk-diversifications, and the polity-market discursive mechanism in development choices gained by evolving technology into higher levels of adaptation, brings about complementarities between the user and the environing entities.

In the case of biodiversity, as a way towards production and cost/risk-diversifications within the dynamic basic-needs regimes of development, the social discursive mechanism evaluates and guides technological change in the direction of meeting the following tests.

Technical efficiency (productivity and cost efficiency), say T1, and social efficiency (adaptation), say S1, of a given technological choice, together determine the well-being function, say $W(T1,S1; \wp)$, such that there exist pervasive complementarities between T1 and S1. The two goals are defined in terms of their respective variables. Between these sets of state and policy variables, there exists circular causation. The end result is simulation of $W(.)$ subject to the circular causation relations between the variables. Such a methodology denotes the ontic (evidential) stage of project evaluation in respect of specific issues and problems under investigation.

The discursive nature of forming knowledge flows on the basis of unity of knowledge is signified by the learning preference map denoted by $\wp$. This is the result of interactive, integrative and evolutionary (IIE) learning among the discourse agents and the multidimensional issues and problems in specific systems that remain under discourse.

6.4   Another Critical Example in Science and Technology in the Framework of Unity of Knowledge: Black Hole

The contrasts between unity of knowledge and rationalism as opposed to the constructs of socio-scientific reality can be continued on the side of pure scientific theories. Take an example here.

Recall that the Hubble Telescope is a technology emanating from the physical theory of Black Holes. The assumption underlying this area of science and technology is that singularities exist in the experiential universe, such as a Black Hole. It denies causality inside it. That is, Black Holes engulf all information about things that fall into it.

Whereas, in the Tawhidi worldview methodology of circular causation and continuity model for understanding pervasive complementarities, there must necessarily exist causality and its measurement *inside* the Black Hole as much as outside it. The theory of Black Hole according to theoretical physics cannot transmit information from inside the event horizon. Thus, a contradiction arises between the nature of knowledge of events and experience between the outside and the inside of the Black Hole. A Black Hole must therefore be defined in a different way that can enable an understanding of unification of systemic knowledge, which explains physical reality by means of pervasive causality and complementarities between entities both outside and inside the Black Hole.

6.4.1   *The E-O-O-E interpretation of Black Hole phenomenon*

On the basis of the E-O-O-E methodology, the two ways of interpreting reality — one by singularity and another by complementarities — contradict each other. Hence, the explanation of theoretical physics is questionable. The technology of the Black Hole must be transformed into such a scientific mindset that provides a unique way of understanding physical reality. The results would lead into agreeable interpretations of observations according to the methodology of E-O-O-E. Such an understanding must apply uniquely to both the outside and inside of the event horizon of the Black Hole.

If we assume multidimensional phenomena space for the Black Hole, then the corresponding scientific ideas would be of the nature of mathematical hyperspaces of abstract entities, and time would be treated as topological time. Such a scientific inquiry will have to abandon the physical constraint based on the principle of invariance of the laws of physics and of the universal constants. These are now subjected to learning and endogenous relationships in the E-O-O-E worldview methodology.

The objective scientific inquiry of Black Hole in such a case would be to develop a process-driven objective criterion in which science and technology are interrelated in the perspective of a unified worldview of reality without singularities. Singularities are space-time states where events do not happen and circular causation relations cannot take place. Scientific relations around singularities are instead reformulated by abandoning the postulate of invariance of physical laws and physical constants in the large and small-scale universes. The Black Hole phenomenon is now redefined so as to accede to systemic causality both inside as well as outside its event horizon. This is a scientific project that is presently not amenable to theoretical physics. On the contrary, scientific explanation of such a unified nature would be premised on the epistemology of unity of knowledge in reference to the E-O-O-E process-driven worldview methodology.

New theoretical investigations have recently been launched that come nearer to exploring alternative definitions of the Black Hole. Firstly, there is the recent lecture by Stephen Hawking (2004) given at the University of Dublin. In it he remarks:

> This loss of information wasn't a problem in the classical theory. A classical black hole would last forever, and the information could be thought of as preserved inside it, but just not very accessible. However, the situation changed when I discovered that quantum effects would cause a black hole to radiate at a steady rate. At least in the approximation I was using, the radiation from the black hole would be completely thermal, and would carry no information. So what would happen to all that information locked inside a black hole that evaporated away, and disappeared completely? It seemed the only way the information could come out would be if the radiation was not exactly thermal, but had subtle correlations. No one has found a mechanism to produce correlations, but most physicists believe one must exist. If information were lost in black holes, pure quantum states would decay into mixed states, and quantum gravity wouldn't be unitary.

Roger Penrose (1989) is pursuing his project on Quantum Gravity, which aims at unifying Relativity Physics and Quantum Physics. In this project, he is arguing along the lines of Hawking regarding the escaped information from the Black Hole. Yet, there is a negative energy caused by a particle that falls into the Black Hole. The question of information resolution still is that the causality between entities inside the Black Hole must be explained to be amenable to analysis. As it stands, even in the Quantum Gravity project, the case of singularity applies to negative energy inside the Black Hole.

6.5   Conclusion

Technology like any other thing is not inherently ethically benign as science would have us believe. The nature of scientific inquiry under the project of unity of knowledge emanating from the episteme of One-ness of God as derived from the Tawhidi worldview in the E-O-O-E knowledge-centered framework can be contrary to mainstream scientific reasoning. The premise of the Tawhidi worldview methodology is unity of knowledge and its end is the same. Hence, a self-referencing methodology is invoked in terms of the proven and most reduced and irreducible premise of knowledge. Once so established by logical and analytical reasoning, it is then possible to make this foundational epistemology the basis of construction of the Universal Paradigm of "everything".

In conclusion to this chapter we raise and answer the question: is the scientific world of ultimate reality near at hand in the modern world-system? We argue out the answer like this.

In terms of production of technological artefacts, there will come about glut and competition in the technology markets. In terms of the new way of thinking along lines of well-being, poverty alleviation, employment and environmental sustainability and the like, these will rarely exist. Governments and international development organizations will try to provision the shortfall, but at high economic, social and political costs. It will be to the interest and benefit of global capitalism to maintain such status quo for serving rent-seeking behavior. Likewise, such policy interventions will be of the exogenous type, enforced without a climate of integration with social realities. The endogenous learning system of discourse and change that goes with learning along lines of unity of knowledge between the agents of change will remain distanced.

For instance, producers of environmental technologies will focus on measures of managerial efficiency for using these to make choices relating to production technologies in the milieu of economic competition. Specific factor ratios will be maintained, causing inflexibility between capital, labor and the environment using capital-using technologies and labor-saving technologies. Such constant factor ratios will point to long-term unchanged technological regimes along the outputs expansion path. This will mark a sign of structural rigidity in technological change.

That is, under modernity as presently conceived, the meaning and scope of technology and technological change in terms of building up the interactive, integrative and dynamic process of evolution by learning between the agents of change will remain distanced. This will be the consequence in the world of high thinking if power and self-interest continue to mark the future of technology and output expansion in the modern context of technology and technological change.

The way out of this scientific limitation and ethical quagmire is to enable communities and nations to learn from interplanetary discourse in new methods and new visions of change for the well-being of all. This future platform rests on the epistemology of systemic unity of knowledge.

Chapter

7

Human Well-Being Adversely Affected by Interest-Based Financing

7.1   Interest, Debt and Human Ecology: Opening the Debate

The holistic concept of human ecology has been misunderstood in the environment debate that assumed international proportion. In human ecology, the vaster domain of the environment is marked by the embedded interaction between society, economy and institutions within the context of sustainability. Sustainability in turn is deeply entrenched in the divine law and guidance calling for unity of the life-sustaining artefacts. Modern thought premised in the age-old development of occidental thought has failed to render this overarching concept of the unity of being. The Universal Paradigm in its world-view framework of unity of the divine law with functional meaning of systems as rendered by *Tawhid* in the Qur'an is the only unique mainstay of the holistic model of human ecology.

Within human ecology, we will discuss the issues of instability of the socioeconomic order caused by such factors as interest financing, debt and inequity. We will establish interrelationships between these and show the consequences on the critical issues from the existing mainstream economic viewpoint and the model of human future in Islam.

In the Western world, consciousness towards a holistic human ecology as a concept in sustainability is only now opening up. Central to this understanding is the need to see the connections between what might — at first sight — appear to be unrelated phenomena. Many connections could be mentioned, but one is of particular relevance to this book — that between the present international banking system and environmental destruction.

7.2   *Riba*/Interest Retards Economic Growth and Development

Consider the following textbook logic. There is an inverse relationship between interest rate and real rate of return. Therefore, if savings increase under the impact of a high interest regime, then all along, the real rates of return in productive outlets will remain low. The investment as opposed to saving implication of the above-mentioned figures is that real rates of return will decline from the first case to the second case. Consequently, real output and rates of return will be discouraged, while savings with higher interest rates continue to be attractive. We have pointed out in the previous chapter that this kind of withdrawal by the route of savings means continuously increasing loss in potential output. The consequences of such adverse financial developments on the social economy were discussed earlier.

Besides, long-term investments will decline and will give way to speculative financial portfolios. This is a proven fact in the global volatile speculative capital markets. Foreign Direct Investments shy away from long-term investments unless such investments are protected by WTO policies such as Trade-Related Investment Measures and Trade-Related Property Rights, and the presently connived Capital Accounts Liberalization (Fischer, 1997). Long-term investments with such WTO protections to large corporations are always to the detriment of the host countries. The political consequences of long-term IMF conditionalities and binding clauses of the WTO can penalize host countries in case of non-compliance with these conditions. Bilateral financial assistances are also severely affected. The most recent instances of hold-up of development assistances by the West are found in the case of Palestine subsequent to Hamas democratic victory and of Sudan in recent times. Libya was spared the sanction only after her ruler, Col. Ghaddafi, surrendered to Western tutelage, and Iraq was invaded by the US, Britain and the Western Alliance.

We further explain the adverse effect of savings caused by the lure of compound interest on debt in this way. Savings accumulated in banks go to build up the excess reserves and the statutory reserves. The excess reserve becomes the source of multiple credit creation by interbank loans. Such loans accumulate as interbank lending proceeds across the economy. Part of this rate is paid to customers as interest to maintain the incentive to save and continue on the saving process. A higher differential is retained with the banks as surpluses from the multiple credit creation generated by interbank interest rates. This is also the answer to the question usually asked: how does idle saving generate interest?

The savings as financial withdrawal at the time it is done causes both a potential loss of output that could otherwise have come from real returns, and it represents contrarily an amount that must now come from multiple credit creation, which generates bank interest related to profit and income. Thus, the interest on the principal is not generated productively. It comes out of "nothing", i.e., as paper money through multiple credit creation. Such interbank and interproject or clientele loans are multiplied by interbank lending at given interest rates to produce compound interest.

7.3   Debt Cycle in the Global Scene

In this section we explain the socioeconomic instability caused by debt cycles in terms of debt ratios such as debt/export ratio and debt/output ratio (Choudhury, 1994). The latter one concerns us more. In turn, these debt ratios are transformed into debt/resource ratios. Resource here comprises flow of capital resources from external and domestic sources as transfers or loans, and of productively generated incomes from reinvestments plus profits generated domestically. Thus, total resource stock is $R = R(D) + R(F) + R(Q) + R(Ln) + R(G)$, where

$R(D)$ denotes resources generated domestically; $R(F)$ denotes external flow of resources; $R(T)$ denotes resources generated by tax revenues; $R(Q)$ denotes resources generated productively, which can be retained earnings that are reinvested; $R(Ln)$ denotes resources from external loans; and $R(G)$ denotes official flows of resources.

In the above identity, there are certain tradeoffs between the resources. For instance, with increasing real output Q, automatic stabilization will call forth an increase in T. Contrarily, increasing T will decrease the real output level. Likewise, increasing Q and T, that is of $R(D)$, will reduce G but will not necessarily reduce Ln. Increased flows in G will decrease Ln by virtue of the fact that G is a transfer to less developing economies. G being a correction factor for development is of the nature of structural adjustment. Hence, G does not finance investments.

An important inference to note from the above tradeoffs is the direction of resource flows in terms of development regimes and factor utilization. In mainstream economic reasoning, such tradeoffs are accepted under the economic assumption of scarcity and competition. In the participatory development framework of the E-O-O-E type, tradeoffs are replaced by pervasive complementarities. In the case of environmental issues, it is the dynamic basic-needs regime, and thereby, participatory development framework, that counts.

7.3.1 *Desired and contrary relations in dynamic basic-needs regimes of development*

In the dynamic basic-needs regime of development, the following kinds of relationships are expected in view of sectoral linkages that involve a central causality with the agricultural sector. Increasing Q requires decreasing T (hence, a "good" tradeoff, for T is treated here as a bad). This implicates a complementary relationship between real Q and lower taxes. Then there are complementary relationships between Q, G and Ln. Finally, over all, complementarities are established between real Q, G, Ln and decreasing T, as more resources are injected in development that is linked intersectorally through the use of the participatory framework. Dynamic basic-needs regimes of development that promote sustainability and environmental sound-ness is an experience in such complementarities. The same result is felt on the side of productive factors in terms of the complementary struc-tural changes that play a critical role in the development of social con-tracts between productive factors within a participatory framework of development.

Furthermore, a dynamic basic-needs regime of development reflects the appropriateness of technological choices in the framework of circular causality relating to user-technology interrelationship that was explained in the previous chapter. Now, an examination of the saving-investment-development interrelationship is in place in refer-ence to the debt question. The issue of debt cycle has to do with such saving-investment-development circular causation interrelationships.

In development regimes with the supply of saving (S) being either higher or lower than the demand for investment (I), there will be either upward pressure on interest rates or interest-rate volatility will appear. These will adversely affect capital market and real economy linkages. We note that the supply of saving (S) is a positive function of sub-potential income level (Q') and the rate of interest (i). Contrarily, the demand for investment is a positive function of potential output (Q) and inverse to 'i'. We have noted this kind of movement in an earlier mention on the accumulation of funds.

When savings exceed investment, potential financial resource withdrawal, and thereby debt, are caused by the financing of the potential output gap. When investment exceeds savings, there is excess demand for funds. Consequently, debt financing and increasing inter-est rate in the face of scarcity of funds draw down investment once again. In between these scenarios, when savings equate to investments, interest rates decrease.

Keynesian macroeconomics refers to this state of the economy as the low-level equilibrium trap with low interest rate and a correspond-ing expansion of potential output. Between these three phases of the economy, interest rates move from a given high level to competition with rates of return on equity, thereby causing financial and output instability and volatility. The stock of capital accumulation fluctuates between bonds and interest-bearing assets, causing instability in finan-cial equities. In recent times, this kind of instability has marked the volatile state of global capital markets. Thereby, the real growth rates of the economies also remain unstable and uncertain.

The middle phase of economic change with savings equating to investments also does not address the issues of productivity and stability. That is because the accumulation at this phase is caused by past savings that were accumulated on the basis of the lure for interest rates (i.e., from the state of $S > I$ or $I > S$). Only if this state is a perpetual occasion for the economy over its lifecycle, then that would indicate full mobilization of resources into productive investments. But the theory and implications of such a dynamic basic-needs regime of development are contrary to the above-mentioned type of business cycle.

7.3.2   *The case of basic-needs regimes of development with resource mobilization*

In the resource mobilization case, debt cycle cannot appear across business cycles, since the incentives on capital formation work out from the productivity side. Together with this, the spending along the path of potential output is in the good things of life. This restricts excesses on the consumer and on the production sides (the Qur'an calls this bad as *Israf* = waste). Consequently, a dynamic basic-needs regime is the logical consequence. Sustainability is caused by the underlying participatory dynamics of the basic-needs regimes of development. As a result, debt cycles are eliminated. The absence of interest rate regimes and its replacement by participatory financing instruments annul debt financing.

There is also an automatic stabilization dynamics here that is causally related with zero debt. In the real economic linkages between financial and physical resource mobilization, sustainable economic development brings about gains in output and spending in the good things of life. This causes productive factors to be mobilized in participatory production venues. Thereby, the quantity of money in the economy complements with spending in the good things of life. Now, the rate of growth of the quantity of money, the rate of growth of prices in the dynamic basic-needs regime of development, and the rate of growth of potential output equal each other.

This is a sure sign of annulment of inflationary pressures. Consequently, interest rates, savings and debt decline together on a trend. Hence, automatic stabilization remains as a perpetually endogenous adjustment during the evolving and learning phases of complementary economic and social relations. This is the meaning of systemic unity of knowledge in the light of the instruments of participation and alleviation of interest caused by appropriate financing instruments and the social consciousness of the moral law.

The sectoral and institutional specific linkages imply such unity of knowledge in the systemic sense. Systemic participation, dynamic preference formation among the agents in such a system of learning relations, and the appropriate policy and financing instruments arising from the underlying episteme of unity of knowledge get implemented in the sense of dynamic basic-needs regimes of development.

7.3.3   *Implications of debt cycle on factor utilization and sustainability*

Since debt cycles are generated by the departures of the Gross Domestic Product from potential output, and thereby, savings form a conflict with resource mobilization, therefore, choices of technology in each of the three phases of business cycle will affect productive factors in specific ways.

Firstly, when $S > I$, an increase in investments by injection of savings will cause interest rates to decline. Consequently, the economy moves towards the phase of $S = I$. Secondly, along the business cycle, higher investments will cause labor-intensive technological choices. From the other side, as $I > S$ moves into the phase of $S = I$, higher interest rates will curtail the investment demand and cause savings to increase. Now, capital-intensive technological choice will be favored. Thirdly, when $S = I$, there is only temporary stability in the economy, for such a phase is still recognizably caused by a history of debt and business cycles. These cases permanently disable the economy even as it attains the state of $S = I$. The economy thereafter moves into unstable economic phases.

Sustainability can happen only when resource mobilization into the ethically generated real economic ventures is maintained by

appropriate interaction between markets and polity. Now, technological change remains to be of the equally factor-augmentation type.
Economic evolution is charted by the expansion of real output, the
expansion of resource mobilization, and by the equally labor and capital factor-augmenting technological choice.

The implication of such economic states for environmental sustainability is this. Dynamic basic-needs regimes of development that
favor environmental and social sustainability are the most appropriate
ones for sustaining the equally labor and capital (and other productive
factors) factor-augmenting technological change. Prices of dynamic
basic-needs remain stable because of the elastic nature of the demand
and supply curves of basic needs. Demand and supply curves shift
upwards under the force of dynamic transformation by systemic learning. Revenue and income are now output elastic at given stable prices.
Therefore, a higher derived demand for all productive factors is possible in a participatory social economy with progressive market-polity
interaction taking place.

In the knowledge-induced learning system driven by the E-O-O-E
dynamics, the points of resource allocation of the participatory economy that address the environmental sustainability issues are mutually
affected by embedded forces. These forces follow the IIE-processes
generated by circular causation between economic output, the technology pertaining to equally labor- and capital-augmenting technological
change, the environment resources and market-polity interaction. All
of these take place on matters concerning complementarities between
the forces at work and are expressed by their representative variables
for quantitative estimation.

7.3.4   Diagrammatic explanation of debt cycles between labor- and capital-intensive regimes of development

Figure 7.1 explains the cycles of debt-creating resource flows as
a developing economy goes through labor-intensive versus capital-
intensive development choices. This implicates the consequences of
choice of these two kinds of technological change in development.

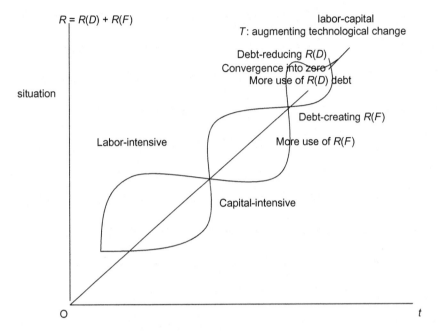

Figure 7.1: Switches and Cycles in Resource Flows and Debt Converging to Equally Labor- and Capital-Augmenting Technological Change

To formalize,

let R denote total resources for socioeconomic development;
$R(F)$ denotes foreign flow of resources;
$R(D)$ denotes domestic flow of resources;
Thereby, $R = R(D) + R(F)$.
Db denotes debt cycle;
L denotes quantities of labor in the labor-intensive technological choice;
K denotes quantity of capital in a capital-intensive technological choice;
OT is the path of evolution of the equally labor- and capital-augmenting development regime. This is also the path of complementarities between labor and capital in the growth model.

Figure 7.1 shows that a labor-intensive technological choice brings about a greater use of $R(D)$, and thereby, a declining reliance on $R(F)$

occurs. Now, external debt is eliminated as $R > R(F)$ along the path of labor-intensive path of socioeconomic development. Conversely, a capital-intensive choice results in a higher dependence on $R(F)$, and thereby, contraction of domestic resource utilization occurs. Debt is now caused by a capital-using technological change through national dependence on $R(F)$. Along the path OT, debt is written off by means of complementarities between labor and capital in the production function of goods and services. That is, now $dR(D)/dt + dR(F)/dt = dR/dt = $ constant. That is,

$$d^2R(D)/dt^2 + d^2R(F)/dt^2 = 0. \tag{7.1}$$

Equation (7.1) implies that with the intensification in the use of domestic resources to curb external debt and gain self-reliant socioeconomic development, any use of $R(F)$ will be less intensive along the path of socioeconomic development. Now, each of the following will be identically zero: $d^2R(D)/dt^2 = 0$; $d^2R(F)/dt^2 = 0$. Thereby, $R(D)$ and $R(F)$ increase by a constant slope over time. It is the role of appropriate policies on technological choice to bring these respective slopes of the trajectories equal to each other. This kind of adjustment is reflected along the path OT. OT is the equally labor- and capital-augmenting path generated by interaction between the state variables, (L, K), and by interaction between the state and policy variables. The two sets of variables bridge the gap between labor-using and capital-using technologies.

Foreign capital is inevitably loaded by interest rates of different term structures. Domestic resources can also be debt-creating by way of interest rates. These resource flows will together result in budgetary deficits.

But along regimes of money-real economy complementarities and balanced budget policies promoting complementarities between labor and capital, together with productive capital market performance linked with the real sectors, convergence occurs. OT is therefore the complementary path of state and policy variables driven by appropriate choices of technologies and social preferences.

7.4   The Connection between Interest-Bearing Money and Environmental Destruction

We return now to the relationship between interest, debt and the environment problem. We have noted above that the reinforcing effect between interest and debt causes an overall human ecological problem, not simply of the environment.

Neoclassical economics makes the argument that financing by environmental financial bonds for protection of the environment can serve as a compensation package. This is flawed reasoning.

Bonds are used to service debt, which in turn depends on the overdrafting of financial resources to finance projects beyond productive means. In this case, savings as withdrawal from potential national output causes continued prevalence of interest rate and debt accumulation. Bonds being a way to raise public money for excess demand for funds in projects are based on announced interest rates. Thus, a double build-up of savings for financing the excess demand beyond the productive capability drives the economy to protracted debt overhang.

Since the real rate of interest can be approximated by the bond rate, we can write

$$R_B = i_N - R_{inf}, \qquad (7.2)$$

where R_B denotes bond rate (approximating to the real rate of interest); i_N denotes nominal rate of interest; and R_{inf} denotes rate of inflation.

During prosperous economic times, R_{inf} and i_N would decline. Now for $R_B > 0$, it must be true that $i_N > R_{inf} > 0$. Consequently, $i_N > R_B$ during economic regimes that bear positive inflation rates. In such a case, to make bonds competitive against bank savings, they must pay a risk premium that adds on to R_B. Such a risk premium is a form of interest rate. It is a cost that arises outside the productive capacity of the economy, and thereby, adds to economic speculation and debt.

7.5   How Would the Praxis of Unity of Knowledge of the Universal Paradigm Address the Environment-Economy-Society Problems?

The environment-economy-society issues are embedded social wholes. Their interactions involve a direct addressing by the sustainability model. We have seen that mainstream economics and treatment of the environment as a depreciable capital asset in it does not address the sustainability issue correctly. The result is always a marginalist tradeoff, as in neoclassical economics, and this postulate is taken over by all branches of mainstream economics. In neoclassical economics, this tradeoff goes by the term marginal rate of substitution or opportunity cost of competing choices.

A critical example of such a choice in the neoclassical growth and development agenda is the tradeoff between economic efficiency (e.g., growth, productivity and price stability) and distributive equity (e.g., social expenditure, employment, environment protection, empowerment and entitlement). The social welfare criterion explaining resource allocation between these competing ends always has in it conflicting variables on opposite sides of the tradeoff.

Contrarily, the E-O-O-E methodology of development planning suggests that pervasive complementarities must exist between the two sides and between the variables representing economy (markets), environment (ecology) and society (institutions and human preferences). The principal argument behind this kind of sustainability caused by linkages and evolutionary learning between the variables is that the agents on each side of the variables come to discourse the common issues and construct a social contract that is mutually consensual between the agents. Here, the moral and ethical laws of the Universal Paradigm are invoked. The episteme of unity of the divine will, its guidance at every level of human consciousness, and the application of these to social details cause the diverse variables to become complementary. The evolutionary result in the emergent learning processes is a release of fresh knowledge flows that reveals possibilities beyond the previous conditions of interaction, integration and evolution between the state variables and institutional variables on the issues under discourse and analysis.

7.6   Characterizing the Production Menu in the E-O-O-E Dynamics

The results on the analytical side are that the output production function in this case comprises productive factors such as labor, capital, and diversity of natural resources, financial resources and policy variables. The policy vector has in it those instruments that inversely relate to interest rates, such as profit and loss sharing, trade financing, joint venture, co-financing, productive charitable resources (*Zakat* in Islam) and communal participatory mechanism (*Shura* in Islam). These cooperative mediums work oppositely to interest rates because each of them acts in favor of production, cost and risk-sharing. These require the fullest scope of resource mobilization into the real economy of the good things of life. The result is that risk diversifies, causing opportunities for further expansion of output, technology and multimarkets of goods and services. In this way, both product-diversification and risk-diversification go hand in hand. Besides, such instruments being of the cooperative kind, they help to reorganize the economy, businesses, enterprises and society along lines of pervasive complementarities between them.

7.7   Conclusion: A Dialectical Question on the Search for the Principle of Pervasive Complementarities in the Light of the Universal Paradigm

It is a matter of critical search to find whether any text other than the Qur'an would have laid down precise guidance and its implements for the epistemology of such a participatory worldview. The answer is that none other exists. The arguments on such a search were presented earlier. Either the premise of rationalism leaves an empty space between truth and falsehood, or there exists no such other divine text that can precisely point out the participatory instruments for human discourse and well-being resting upon the primary guidelines and their functioning.

In all of these, the preferences built upon avoidance of resource waste (*Israf* in the Qur'an, an example being interest denoting undue excess as waste of potential output and factor productivity) and pairing (e.g., recycling, reusing) play critical roles. Such a unified preference map was earlier denoted by $\wp$ in terms of the knowledge-inducing effect generated by the IIE-processes between the group-specific preferences arising from the sides of economy (markets), environment (resource sustainability), and policy variables (institutions). The effectiveness in realizing sustainability in such an IIE-process methodology is attained by the following direction of causality. The reference to the E-O-O-E model is now made with the symbols as defined earlier:

Process 1   **Continuously Simulative Processes**

$$(\Omega, S) \ni \{\theta\} \to (\theta, \mathbf{X}(\theta)) \to \wp(\theta, \mathbf{X}(\theta)) = \cup_{f} \cap_{i} \wp_{ij}(\{\theta, \mathbf{X}(\theta)\})$$

$$\downarrow$$

$$\to M(\theta, \mathbf{X}(\theta); \wp(\theta, \mathbf{X}(\theta)))$$

$$\downarrow$$

$$W(\theta, \mathbf{X}(\theta); \wp(\theta, \mathbf{X}(\theta)))$$

Subject to circular causation
between the variables → ….. Closure in Ω

Here, $(\theta, \mathbf{X}(\theta))$ denotes the bundle of the economy-environment-society variables induced by knowledge and preferences developed in response to the model of the real world, as provided in the ideal epistemological text. Upon this, the moral law $M(.)$ is established and the world-system (economy-environment-society embedding) generated to actualize well-being $W(.)$, subject to pervasive complementarities between the state variables and the policy variables. Both of these kinds of variables are included in $\mathbf{X}(\theta)$. Among the policy variables are the inverse indicators between rates of return on participatory productive enterprises and the interest rate. Consequently, bank savings and bonds are automatically phased out. Spending in the good things of life (ecology, poverty alleviation and sustainability) is encouraged to gain productive capacity.

Chapter

8

Problems of Economic Reasoning and the Islamic Panacea

To exemplify the problem undertaken here, we return to the relationship between interest, debt and the environment problem. We have noted previously that the reinforcing effect between interest and debt causes an overall human ecological problem, not simply of the environment.

Neoclassical economics makes the argument that financing by environmental financial bonds for protection of the environment can serve as a compensation package. This is flawed reasoning.

Bonds are used to service debt, which in turn depends on the over-drafting of financial resources to finance projects beyond productive means. In this case, savings as withdrawal from potential national output causes continued prevalence of interest rate and debt accumulation. Bonds being a way to raise public money for excess demand for funds in projects are based on announced interest rates. Thus, a double build-up of savings for financing the excess demand beyond the productive capability drives the economy to protracted debt overhang.

8.1 Recasting the New Way to Economics and World-Systems in the Universal Paradigm of Unity of Knowledge

The intention in this section is to inquire into the methodological premise that negates not only neoclassical economic theory, but also the entire mainstream economics. We will also cover a criticism of the area termed as social economics to show the emptiness of this way of economic reasoning. Yet, because of the limitation of space, the coverage of none of these three criticisms will be exhaustive. We will touch on a few aspects of these to bring out the total reversal of economic thinking away from the mainstream way in the Universal Paradigm.

Recall here the comment made by Arrow (see Feiwel, 1987) on the need for methodology in developing economics in any way, be this by science or rhetoric (McCloskey, 1985). Arrow (in Feiwel, p. 45) writes,

> Though we have been taught to distinguish sharply between the "is" and the "ought", the logical analysis of decisions tends to blur the lines between them. The distinction can, and in my judgment should be kept, but it requires great clarity of thought to do so.

Thus, the challenge of mature and sublime thought is to construct such an abiding worldview premised on such an epistemological source that can uphold the reasoning, test and application to the maximum number of issues and problems encountered. This Universal Paradigm ought to accomplish these tasks by making recourse to such a unique worldview that remains universal in all disciplines. We have categorized such a Universal Paradigm in the model of E-O-O-E regarding unity of knowledge in learning systems according to the analytics of self-referencing methodology of the divine text.

Institutional economics left behind a legacy of contra-neoclassical thinking. During its early times, American institutionalism under Veblen, Mitchell, Ayres and others was instrumental in bringing about the New Deal on American Social Security. Yet, over the years, institutionalism failed to gain credence in the intellectual circles. The reason for this was the lack of analytical content in institutional economics. Much of institutional economics was policy analysis and rhetoric. Thus, even in the face of institutionalism, neoclassical economics continued to gain grounds. Today, new institutionalism, public choice theory and social contractarianism are being explained by the self-same neoclassical methodology because of the lack of any new methodological development in the intellectual economic circles.

8.1.1   Criticism of neoclassical economics by the methodology of the Universal Paradigm

We have already established the contrast between the axiom (principle) of pervasive complementarities according to the epistemology of unity of knowledge and the marginalist hypothesis of mainstream economics comprising both microeconomics and macroeconomics (Dasgupta, 1987). Here, we will apply this contrast to themes such as resource, markets, institutions, preference formation and production menus. The E-O-O-E model is once again invoked.

The Principle of Pervasive Complementarities rests upon the capability of learning among all interacting, integrating and evolutionary organisms in the socio-scientific world-systems. That this is always the case as the intrinsic nature of continuous change defines a true characteristic of reality. Contrarily, there being nothing in the organic nature of world-systems that remains unmoved, therefore, the postulate of marginal substitution (tradeoff), scarcity, competition, optimality and steady-state equilibrium are fabricated axioms of reality, made to solve problems by assumptive nicety and controlled experimentation.

The fact that nothing in the universe remains independent of learning, explains the function of time as a derivative of knowledge flows emanating from the realization of unity of knowledge in world-systems. Contrarily, in mainstream economics, change is a function of time primarily. Time is the exogenous entity of change. In this sense, knowledge flows arising from the epistemic origin are also functions of time. Yet, in all of these arguments, time is both exogenous, independently introduced and is a perceptual entity.

The clear example of the limitation of defining change and learning as functions of time is to note that the nature of resource allocation, the axioms of scarcity, competition, optimality and steady-state equilibrium remain invariant over time. Thereby, time simply reorganizes such entities in structurally invariant forms. Institutions thereby become benign to structural change. Policies cause distortions in the optimal allocation of resources, but not by structural transformation either in the way of thinking or its implementation in the real world. The reality of cultural, political and embedded forces remains absent and is forgotten in the optimal resource allocation regime of mainstream economics.

Human and institutional preferences are assigned as datum for the benefit of generating predictable behavior and decisions. Dynamic learning preferences are thereby non-existent, except for states of reorganization of the Pareto-optimal resource allocation positions into new sets of Pareto-optimal ones. Both process and organism are absent in such non-interactive and non-learning preference maps.

Contrarily, upon invoking the Principle of Pervasive Complementarities, we note that there is no static resource allocation point, because of continuous learning by the IIE-process between entities. Hence, such neoclassical concepts as opportunity cost, marginal rate of substitution, relative prices determined by optimal production possibility surface, utility function, production function and the associated relations relating to optimization objective criteria cannot exist.

The resource allocation issue of neoclassical economic theory is replaced by distributional paths in the light of the continuous IIE-processes that must be sustained between state and institutional variables by discourse, participation and interrelationships. Thereby, the expansion path under such governance between market forces and institutions determines the distributional perspectives of goods and productive factors. But such an expansion path of a participatory economy, being perturbed by knowledge-induced IIE-process-driven decisions, are subjected to probability estimation in approximating a most probable path out of the bundle of multiple possibilities.

Now, every point along multiple learning resource allocation trajectories gets embedded in a field of complex organism. Within this field of complexity, a mathematical expected vector value of the learning points converges in the domain by consensual decisions. Yet, because of continuous learning caused by IIE-processes between the entities of the domain, even the convergent expected value of the vector of embedded values is not fully attained. The expected equilibriums so estimated in the probabilistic sense get further evolved by continuous learning in the proximity of convergent vector values. They are referred to as evolutionary equilibriums (Choudhury, 2006; Choudhury, Zaman and Al-Nassar, forthcoming 2007).

In the end, the expansion path of output and of productive factors in terms of their IIE-relations with other variables, including prices and policy variables, is determined by the simulation of the Social Well-Being Criterion, subject to circular causation between the representative variables.

The simulation system of the E-O-O-E framework now reaches the ontic (evidential) stage of completion of a process in the IIE-processes that characterizes the dynamics of the Universal Paradigm. The distributional as opposed to the allocative problems between outputs and factors are now solved by establishing better states of complementarities between the variables relating to the particular circular causation equations that deal with the outputs and productive factors. Marginal substitution postulate of neoclassical resource allocation problem is replaced by pervasive complementarities generated along IIE-processes. These continue on in terms of the state and institutional variables and their social well-being evaluation.

The expansion path, better referred to as the History (Choudhury, 2004), reflects a learned experience attained by knowledge induction along the simulation model of the IIE-processes. Hence, it denotes a factual and realistic simulated path of the real world in the presence of knowledge induction and the embedded world-systems. In the present case, the markets are embedded in varieties of systems.

In all of mainstream economics, pronouncedly in neoclassical economics, resource allocation and determination of relative prices of goods and services are done on the basis of marginal rates of substitution; whereas, in the participatory economy with the Principle of Pervasive Complementarities prevailing, relative prices arise from the demand and supply relations of multimarkets that are interrelated. Yet, we note below the different nature of demand and supply equilibriums in the two perspectives — that is, of mainstream economic reasoning and the epistemological reasoning of the Universal Paradigm.

8.1.2   *Evolutionary equilibriums: How to determine relative prices according to the principle of pervasive complementarities*

In mainstream microeconomics, market equilibrium is either a static or a steady-state time-dependent dynamic point of market adjustment. There is no idea of process underlying such change (Shackle, 1971). Only time reveals the change or shifts in market equilibriums as demand and supply schedules shift under the impact of exogenous factors. But when time is made to impact upon such change, then we encounter the econometric problem of identification in estimating demand and supply functions. In every case, the market adjustment processes remain silent on the complexity of market-polity interaction. Thereby, consumer preferences and supplier menus remain fixed, once these are assigned to such given schedules. As mentioned earlier, this is a nicety that is required to make economic consequences of a predictable nature under simplified axioms. Yet, such simplifications do not represent market reality.

The microeconomic multimarket equilibriums in embedded fields of IIE-processes between state and policy variables define probability fields existing around certain points of consensus developed by participation between entities and agents. The latter are represented by their state and policy variables. Such probabilistically converged points are not "attained", but rather, approximated in the face of evolutionary learning. This was explained earlier in reference to the idea of History. Now, the gyrating Cobweb equilibrium points of market adjustments that we find in microeconomics are transformed into evolutionary learning points. They are interpreted in probabilistic concept by the force of continuous knowledge induction occurring in knowledge-induced space-time continuums. Such probabilistic convergent points represent embedded pairing of state and policy variables. The paired variables were earlier described as the topological tuple,

$$Z(\theta^*, \mathbf{X}^*(\theta^*)) = \{\theta^*, \mathbf{X}^*(\theta^*); \wp(\theta^*, \mathbf{X}^*(\theta^*))$$
$$= \cup_i \cap_j \wp_{ij}(\theta^*, \mathbf{X}^*(\theta^*))\}; \tag{8.1}$$
$$d\theta^*/d\theta > 0; \quad (\theta, \theta^*) \in \Omega.$$

The symbols in expression (8.1) were defined earlier. Here, $(\theta^*, \mathbf{X}^*(\theta^*)) = \text{Expected } \{\theta, \mathbf{X}(\theta)\}$, such that θ^* continues to remain evolutionary with fresh rounds of interaction i following systemic convergence by interaction among j number of system entities. Over the entire range of such evolving interaction and integration, there are continuums of preferences generated by such relational orders. Such dynamic preferences are denoted by $\wp_{ij}(.)$, for which there is a temporary convergence, denoted by $\wp$.

With these characterizations of multimarkets and embedded relational fields of learning entities, we now define the economy (Debreu, 1959) as the collection of all markets in a certain sense of aggregation generated by knowledge induction in the participatory economic order, given resources, preferences and their evolutionary learning capacity.

We write all these facts as:

$$E\{Z(\theta^{**}, \mathbf{X}^{**}(\theta^{**})); R((\theta^{**}, \mathbf{X}^{**}(\theta^{**}))), \wp^{**}(\theta^{**}, \mathbf{X}^{**}(\theta^{**}))\}. \qquad (8.2)$$

Here, $R(.)$ denotes resources generated by the same kinds of IIE-processes between the variables as shown. The double asterisks imply aggregation according to the meaning of complex knowledge induction for the economy-wide case of systemic embedding in IIE-process-based History.

8.1.3   *Nature of goods and services in E-O-O-E framework of markets*

Debreu (1959) remarked that apparently similar goods or services that are distributed over time and space change their identity as similar goods or services. That is, such goods and services get differentiated and their markets are different. In the same way, since knowledge flows perpetually induce goods and services in the participatory embedded market and economic systems, they are always differentiated categories.

Two consequences of such a result are obvious. First, in the dynamic basic-needs regime of development, which is the primary feature of participatory economy under the episteme of unity of knowledge, the knowledge-induced (ethicized) goods are evolutionary in the price, quantity and knowledge geometric quadrant. The result then is that the demand and supply schedules for such goods become elastic but not perfectly elastic, as is otherwise the case of classical markets of basic needs.

Consequently, there is always the incentive on the part of sellers and consumers to gain in their revenues and well-being, respectively, as the History of knowledge-induced price and quantity evolutions remains stable throughout the lifecycle of the economy. Moreover, such price and quantity stability is felt throughout multimarkets in the participatory economic order. That is so, because all goods (or contrary to "bads") remain complementary ones. Now, relative prices evolve under the impact of knowledge flows across learning History in the same directions. Each set of prices in multimarkets is determined by the above-mentioned demand and supply configurations. Likewise, the quantities of goods (or inverse of "bads") remain monotonic to price stability along the path of economic expansion; that is, along the learning path referred to as History.

Besides, such goods and services, because of their continuous induction by knowledge, feed into production diversification. Production diversification in turn enhances knowledge flows, and thereby increases the intensity of shareholding in partnership. Expansion of production diversification and shareholding diversify unit risk of the shareholders, while spending in the good things of life with price and output stability, increases. This combined feature of product diversification and risk diversification is true of both idiosyncratic risk (business risk) and systemic risk (economy-wide). The latter comes about due to the similar interlinked nature of goods and their complementarities expressed through prices and quantities in multimarkets.

Goods of the type we are considering here are included in the vector of variables, $X(\theta)$. Thus, a good and service now exists in its integrated two parts, the soul denoted by θ, and the body denoted by X, hence the symbol $X(\theta)$ (Dewitt, 1992).

Such a good and service has recently been referred to in the literature as spiritual good (capital) (Zohar and Marshall, 2004). The good and service and the multimarkets in which they are transacted are ethical and responsible institutions governed and driven by the force of ethical preferences $\wp$, which was explained earlier. In accordance with our earlier explanation of the derivation of the ethical law from its moral foundation, the knowledge induction followed by ethical preferences and economic transformation rest fundamentally upon the precise epistemological foundations. In this work, we have established that epistemological foundation to be the unity of knowledge premised on the divine law guiding reason, precepts and applications to diverse issues of world-systems. This is also the foundational premise of the Universal Paradigm.

8.1.4 *The concept of efficiency, productivity and values in spiritual goods*

The theory of cost and production of social goods as opposed to spiritual goods is associated with total efficiency concept, social productivity and a concept of value that is still tied to social prices. Each of these concepts, well-known in the literature, is a linearly additive one. Private cost is added up with social cost to yield the total cost, so that social cost of production is treated in the similar framework of average and marginal cost. Marginal private costs must equate to marginal social cost to determine optimal pricing and resource allocation in social goods. The productivity concept too is associated with a lateral addition of the factor use in the production of private and social goods. Consequently, it is only logical that in such a case, the production menus of private and social goods exist independently. The concept of value is associated with the marginal social welfare function, which is well-known to be a combination of opposing private and public (social) goods and services that get subjected to marginal resource allocation concept.

All the above facts are true in the case of neoclassical economics and its transference into aggregate production menus. On the other hand, in classical economic theory, value in terms of price is determined by a concept of *jus pretium* (just price). In determining such a concept of value, non-market forces are exogenously introduced. They affect market prices. The role of knowledge as an interactive, integrative and learning force never exists in any of the above concepts in mainstream and classical Enlightenment economics. The ethical preferences remain outside the endogenous role of learning interrelationships between state variables and policy variables, with appropriate guidance and policy instruments premised on unity of knowledge and applied to the participatory social and economic systems.

In the E-O-O-E model of unity of knowledge, the IIE-process methodology gives the fundamental structure of learning. It is the carrier of the Principle of Universal Complementarities and evolutionary learning between entities. In this framework, the concept of efficiency is derived from the average cost-of-production formula expressed by a learning-by-doing curve that remains perpetually under the impact of learning in continuum. Hence, all the probabilistic conditions of evolutionary market equilibriums along the path of economic History remain intact in the simulation of the learning average cost curve. The average cost function, and thereby, the average cost curve in the framework of learning, are better analyzed mathematically than diagrammatically in just two variables, namely quantity and average cost.

The production menu in E-O-O-E is structurally different and opposed to that in mainstream microeconomics and macroeconomics. Now, it represents a social contract combining market and polity factors toward organizing the modes and means of production by complementarities. The marginal rate of substitution between productive factors is abandoned. The neoclassical microeconomic and macroeconomic forms of the production possibility frontier and the production isoquants are benign to policies and interaction. No process is implicated in arriving at the optimal resource allocation points. Consequently, only exogenous effects drive the expansion path outwards.

In the E-O-O-E model, under the impact of circular causation and continuity relations between the productive factors, and the state and policy variables, evolution is caused by evolutionary learning. Here, the kind of probabilistic dynamics explained earlier applies. All the deductions in respect of relative (factor) pricing in complementary multimarkets for services hold.

We must clarify one important point here. The fact that the Principle of Pervasive Complementarities fully determines all markets and resource distribution by sharing and augmenting does not mean that some factors cannot have relatively smaller rate of change in its use and incomes. The important point contrarily is to note that any such resource distribution point is determined by the IIE-process methodology, and is thereby, a learning point. Consequently, the probabilistic dynamics of evolutionary learning under unity of knowledge — between entities, systems, state variables and policy variables — apply in repeated continuums. A resource distribution point is therefore always a probabilistic scatter, while that of optimal economics is steady-state equilibrium. Knowledge induces the evolution of resource distribution points, and time is recursively tied to knowledge flows. Time records a particular set of knowledge flows and their induced events; time does not cause knowledge flows and events. Steady-state points are benign to knowledge perturbations. Only evolutionary learning equilibriums matter.

8.1.5   *Productivity concept in IIE-process methodology*

The productivity concept of mainstream economics is simply a static concept of average output per unit of a specific factor, keeping all other factors constant. In the E-O-O-E model, the unique body-soul existence of every vector of variables causes output to be determined by circular causation in terms of one another and their relations explaining knowledge flows.

In the case of optimal economics, optimal factor productivity level yields the result:

Rate of change of output = Rate of change of specific factor use.

$$(8.3)$$

For the E-O-O-E model, no *optimal* factor productivity exists. Factor productivity, like any other variables and the Social Well-Being Criterion, is simulated. Besides, effective organization of the market process with its institutional interface yields positive gains to producers and consumers. Thereby, each of the rates in expression (8.3) is a complex function interrelating knowledge-induced variables.

Now,

Rate of change of output > Rate of change of specific factor use.

$$(8.4)$$

For the case of intertemporal resource allocation and resource distribution in the two contrasting cases, the yield in real assets is computed in contrary ways. In mainstream economics, such a rate is the discount factor for future cash flows. Hence, it is a shadow price, not the real price of scarcity as neoclassical economics would like it to be. All discount rates are therefore time-value of money. Hence, they are of the category of financial interest, and thereby, contrary to the formation of participatory economic, social and ethical relations premised on the divine law of oneness (complementary relations). Contrarily, the rate of return on real assets cannot be calculated by any form of the neoclassical perceived discounting formula.

Instead, a forward intergeneration resource allocation model can be used (Choudhury, 2004). Each point of evolutionary learning in such a model induces knowledge and valuation by knowledge simulation. We have dwelled on this issue profusely in this work.

The concept of economic value as marginal utility, price and *jus pretium* is replaced in the E-O-O-E model by the following concept. Let M denote the intrinsic value in a good. No labor and capital is required to produce this element of value. First, we note that M is non-cognitive. With M in place, the true value of labor and capital imputed in the production and marketing of the good determined on the basis of average cost and factor productivity, say P, must be discounted by M. The effective price as value of the good that enters the well-being function is $p = P - M$.

The question then is this: how is M determined? In answer, we note that price and quantity (as every entity) are determined now solely in a market exchange that remains perpetually under two interactive, integrative and evolutionary learning forces. These forces are caused by circular causation interrelationships between state variables and institutional variables. Preferences and menus are thereby determined, and ethical transformation conveyed to the exchange mechanism. Thus, values underlying the ethics of price moderation caused by the conscious awareness of M, though not in measured terms, enter human behavior through human preference formation. Through such learning preferences, the ethicizing market process is injected and defined, as in expression (8.1). Such a market process endogenizes value formation as realized by $\wp(\theta, \mathbf{X}(\theta))$, as defined. Prices now reveal the ethicizing market mechanism in respect of the value now induced in p.

8.1.6   *Price extensions in IIE-process methodology*

The concept of labor theory of value of mainstream economics is dispensed with, since wages are now subjected to the same kind of ethical and conscious determination as prices in ethicizing market exchange. The combination of labor and capital in value determination too is rejected, since factor payments in this case are also determined in ethicizing factor markets and by the principle of pervasive complementarities between labor and capital, and thereby among all productive factors that are engaged in the production of the life-sustaining goods and services (ethicizing markets). Nowhere in all such determinations can the postulate of marginal rate of substitution, i.e., opportunity cost, hold.

The existence of $p = P - M$ reflects the nature of development and market regimes — dynamic basic needs. Consequently, the prices resulting from the knowledge-induced spiritual goods (capital and labor) in market exchange are lower and stable in the E-O-O-E model than in the mainstream model. The classical notion of price and quantity is abandoned for reasons of their non-learning nature.

Lastly, we note that unlike the idea of marginal utility, marginal social welfare and marginal productivities of mainstream economics, the well-being function of E-O-O-E model expresses complementarities either actual or knowledge-induced through polity-market interaction. Consequently, contrary to the marginal indicators that are benign of interaction, the elasticity coefficients of the well-being function in IIE-process methodology with respect to any set of variables in the learning process is a complex estimable relationship. It is amenable either to observation for reconstruction of complementarities between the knowledge-induced variables (Choudhury and Hossain, forthcoming 2007) or to observer value consciousness.

8.2   The Impossibility of Macroeconomics Everywhere

Ethics in market process is of the essence in reconstructing the value induction in prices, quantities and all economic variables. This leads to the questions on the problems of macroeconomics, and the new study of aggregation in the light of complex learning behavior caused by interaction between state and polity variables along IIE-processes.

Let us briefly examine Keynesian macroeconomics. Keynes consistently thought of saving in all its forms as an economic withdrawal, and thus, a de-multiplier to the growth of output. Spending was an injection, and thus, favorable to the growth of output. Consequently, the two sectors, one supported by saving and the other supported by productive spending in all its forms, become competing, marginal substitutes of each other.

While this is overly emphasized in Keynesian economics, what is worthy of note is the particular understanding of the relationship between saving, capital formation and output over time. The neoclassical and classical roots of Keynes" thought relent toward the marginal substitution principle at the aggregate level of economic analysis. Note that the substitution principle is very damaging for the saving hypothesis. In neoclassical economic theory, saving forms the foundation of capital accumulation. Interest income derived from saving over time becomes the source of wealth formation. In Keynesian thought, spending and the real economy are the sources of output, and hence of wealth formation.

Keynes saw in under full-employment equilibrium an unethical social state. He wished to solve this problem through the presence of government policies to borrow and finance resource mobilization (Saving = Investment) so as to bring the economy to its full-employment level. Also, he saw this to happen at the lowest possible interest rate (low-level liquidity trap). Thus, if an economy is to be sustained under full-employment level of equilibrium, the ethical factor must mobilize financial resource continuously and fully into productive spending.

O'Donnell (1989, p. 164) writes on Keynes' ethical vision relating to ethics and economics:

> Keynes' goal was the development of an ethically rational society consciously tending towards higher levels of goodness; and economics, like all moral sciences, was an instrument in its attainment.

Keynes' concept of full-employment output attained through productive spending, as opposed to savings as withdrawal, was one such envisioned state of ethical relationship in and with economics.

Yet, with all such ethical concerns, where did Keynesian economics and its neoclassical synthesis go wrong? The problem lay in the absence of well-defined preferences, the carriers of ethical consciousness. The absence of a robust theory of dynamic preferences in macroeconomics, and hence the problem of preference aggregation, except by the constancy and identity assumption, causes all treatment of ethical values to become exogenous or benign.

We are then in an analytical dilemma. Microeconomics treats preferences as being prescribed and exogenously given to a resource allocation problem of economic rationality, scarcity, equilibrium and optimization. Macroeconomics is silent on preference aggregation due to the different nature of aggregation in macroeconomics from microeconomics. Thus, in either of these systems, the role of process and discourse is merely implied. They are not endogenously determined and regenerated by systemic synergy.

The ethical insensitivity caused by the absence of endogenous preference formation and of a discursive process in decision-making at both the microeconomic and macroeconomic levels goes deeper into the policy domain. Due to the exogenous nature of preferences and the absence of a process in decision-making, the policy and institutional-presence also enter economic theory with the same characteristics. We have argued earlier that institutional-level preference formation in economic theory means simply a lateral aggregation of individual preference according to the postulate of methodological individualism. Consequently, such other variables as policy, technology, population and social variables remain outside of endogenous preferences. This permanent nature of economic theory, more so observed in macroeconomics, causes its complete ineptness to address ethical issues, except exogenously.

8.3   Critique of Social Economics

The discontent with these failings of mainstream economics led the so-called social economists to question and search in different directions. But here too, either the methodology of analysis or the rigor of an alternative analysis did not exist. Consequently, social economics either treated ethical values as exogenous forces or as cursory changes in received mainstream economic theory, or as rhetoric of economics. None of these worked out because of their inability to reexamine the socio-scientific world-systems with economics being embedded in it, from a new epistemological outlook, when the old ones have failed.

The school of Physiocracy upheld the role of *jus divinum* (divine law) in economic matters, and thereby, dealt with the problems of political economy, even with a certain degree of rigor. The rest of the developments in economic theory remained ambivalent to ethics and were methodologically incapable of integrating ethics with economic issues. In the classical and neoclassical schools, the problem of determining value remained distanced by their peculiar methodology. Marxist economic thought suffered from the problem of price determination in terms of "use value" and "surplus value". Keynes faced a similar problem by being unable to define ethical preference formation in macroeconomic aggregation. The institutional economists could not develop a firm policy-theoretic basis and relied on other received economic thoughts. It is therefore not sufficient to think only ethically regarding just prices, full-employment output and prices, appropriate technology, sustainable development, poverty alleviation, justice, empowerment and entitlement and similar issues. It must be the task of the social economic theory and its applications to endogenously generate, then establish and sustain these primary conditions of well-being. The E-O-O-E model gives the methodology of endogenous integration of ethics in as much as there is market determination of prices and quantities. The E-O-O-E model of the Universal Paradigm genre provides this substantive alternative worldview and its scientific methodology.

8.4   Examples of Spiritual Goods in E-O-O-E Model

Examples of the kinds of ethical goods and services as dynamic basic needs span the entire material basket and development regimes in E-O-O-E model along its IIE-processes. Education, environment, justice, poverty alleviation, affordable housing, avoidance of luxury cars, food availability for reducing hunger, medical services, etc., are just some of the entire range of the material basket that can now be induced by knowledge flows to transform into ethicizing markets. The understanding of global ethics emanating from the moral law, as opposed to humanism of the rationalist process (Lutz and Lux, 1988), determines the correctness of decisions arising from the unique episteme of unity of divine knowledge, the irreducible premise of reality.

On the side of spiritual capital, the most prominent one is interest-free finance and money. This will require deep thinking on the side of relational epistemology governing money, real economy, ethicizing markets, commercial banks and the central bank with the proper forms of instruments, institutions and preference changes. These are issues for deeper investigation in Chapter 9.

8.5 Conclusion

This chapter has shown that the new paradigm of the socio-scientific field, within which is the embedded phenomenon of market mechanism, assumes a deeply rigorous study in the Universal Paradigm, as opposed to all of mainstream economics. The empirical viability of these alternative ways of conceptualizing and estimating the real world events is far more powerfully established in the E-O-O-E model than in the nice but unreal analytics of mainstream microeconomics and macroeconomics. Indeed, there are subtle and damaging contradictions between theory and reality in these latter disciplines.

The two worldviews of the socio-scientific world-systems within which is economics, are opposed to each other. Their methodologies and implications are different. Their epistemological premises are opposed to each other. Mainstream economics and science are derived from the epistemology of rationalism. This has resulted in mainstream economic axioms of perfect knowledge and economic rationality.

Contrarily, the foundations of economics, society and science in the Universal Paradigm are derived from the most reduced premise of the divine law accommodated by reason. This is done methodologically by the self-referencing of the divine law through methodology, verification and interpretation. Upon these bases are constructed the mechanism for interpreting and organizing all issues and problems of world-systems around the epistemology of unity of knowledge.

The compartmentalizing of economics into a narrow discipline is now replaced by the rise of the moral and ethical laws of systemic unity across learning systems. Markets, economics, society, political economy and world-system studies are turned into holistic projects when governed by the E-O-O-E model. We proceed further in this direction in the subsequent chapters.

Chapter

9

Problems of Financial Reasoning and the Islamic Alternative

9.1   Some Technical Issues Interrelating Money, Finance and Resource Mobilization

What do we actually mean when we assert the fact that "money is created as paper"? This has to do with the particular relationship between the central bank, the commercial banks and the real economy. There are certain concepts underlying the explanation of the complementary linkages here that need to be understood and differentiated from the way mainstream economics and finance treats money, finance and real economy circular causation.

The concepts we need to tackle are demand and supply of money, and the quantity of money. Furthermore, there is a difference in the concept of the quantity of money from the way it is used in the monetary literature and the way we will be using it in this chapter in relation to the real economy (Friedman, 1989; Choudhury and Hoque, 2004).

9.1.1   *Demand for money*

The concept of demand for money is linked with the motives that make households hold money. Keynes identified these motives, and which we continue to accept in mainstream economics today, as the transaction demand, the precautionary demand and speculative demand.

Transaction demand equals the money in circulation and is in demand to finance household spending. Likewise, on the basis of cash balances, this household demand for money becomes the receipt of revenue in cash flows to firms who receive them through their sales. Transaction demand for money thereby equals all money in circulation.

Precautionary demand for money is based on part circulation and part savings. The savings part is determined by the lure of interest rates to households. Now, all the problems that we noted with the idea of savings in relation to resource withdrawal, loss of potential output, loss of full-employment and prosperity, entitlement failure, failure in poverty alleviation and capital market instability, can be recalled.

The part of precautionary demand that finances output causes suboptimal levels of national income. The precautionary demand component increases in volume with increases in interest rates, as there is a tradeoff between bank interest rate and the return on shares and the price of bonds. But since bonds also pay interest rates, being a mode of debt financing, therefore, both bank and bond interest rates increase with the increase in the prime rate of the central bank, and thus, by the lure for savings by households.

Lastly, the speculative component of the demand for money is a gamble. Rich savers like to play gamble in capital markets by purchasing speculative papers that are directly under the mercy of a structure of many interest rates. Such a term structure of interest rates made up of various portfolio interest rates and with different time denominations, exchanged nationally and globally, makes the capital markets volatile.

A part of the speculative demand also flows into national output, but this proportion is small in relation to the increased proportion of incomes that are driven into gambles after all discretionary spending is done. The part of the national output generated by speculative demand arises from the financial sector. Two forces thus work oppositely in the relationships between interest rate, financing and output in the real economy.

Firstly, the financial sector and the real economy conflict with each other in response to the fluctuations in the term structure of interest rates of financial gambles. The higher the term structures of interest rates, the more the direction of output into savings and speculation. The less of output thereby flows into productive spending in the real economy. The kinds of capital market instruments that prosper are bonds and interest-bearing secondary ones. Equities become volatile in the process. When equity investments are pursued, they occur in mutual funds. These are hybrids between equities and interest-bearing instruments.

Secondly, the prosperity of the economy declines. Now, there is both economic instability and social deprivation. A just and fulfilling economy ceases to exist, giving way to losses in incomes, causing unemployment, heightened economic insecurity and poverty.

Thirdly, we must emphasize here that withdrawal of potential resources away from the real economy goes into those avenues that do not promote the good things of life. Poverty is abhorred; yet, the rise of speculative demands in the financial sector holdings increases inequity, and thereby poverty and deprivation. It is therefore important to note here that spending in the real economy must be in productive, good things of life. Mere spending in anything, and thereby, in unethical artefacts, does not engender a stable and sustainable economy.

Take the case of overspending, which creates debt and all its economic and social miseries that we have examined earlier. Likewise, spending in luxury goods is a withdrawal of resources from social commons such as affordable housing, fresh water, healthcare and conservation, education, human resource, etc. Higher taxes on luxury goods do not work in favor of social equity, because they are internalized in the decisions of the rich spender on his luxury goods. Our earlier discussion on spiritual goods (capital) in relation to the relevant concepts and measures of efficiency and productivity can be recalled.

When the total demand for money is now accounted for, we note that this is determined by conflicting forces in the economy. The financial sector is governed by volatile term structure of interest rates and savings therefrom. National income generated therefrom does not reflect prosperity, stability and equitable distribution of income and wealth. The real economic sectors are marginalized as the capital market speculation gains momentum, and savings increase as opposed to spending in the good and productive things of life in different outlets.

In summary, the concept of money demand as seen by Tobin (1958) through the neoclassical lens is determined by a marginal substitution (tradeoff) between the opposing forces of stocks and cash balances. Since stocks are based on real rates of return and cash balances on the basis of the bank rate of interest, financial resources get moved in uncertain ways between these ends.

Some have presented the futile argument (Khan and Mirakhor, 1989; Khan, 1991) that in a profit-sharing financial system and the real economy arrangement, the interest rate in capitalizing a bond could be changed mechanically to a real rate of return while keeping the asset valuation formula the same. Thereby, the capitalization formula for bonds according to these authors can be retained, as in the case of time-value of money. This argument is far from the truth.

The fact of the matter is that any form of time-value of money is a shadow rate of interest. Thereby, all the relations of the central bank, the commercial banks, the financial sector and the real economy remain structurally intact, as in the case of the interest-bearing neoclassical economic system. The essence of the money-real economy linkage argument is lost in fiasco by the weak arguments centering on Tobin's q-theory and the neoclassical-type financial asset valuation models (Choudhury and Hoque, 2004).

9.1.2   *Supply of money*

Like the concept of demand for money, that of the supply of money is premised on money being viewed as a commodity. Money as stock is thereby understood as fiat money. Kahf (1992) continues to identify money in Islam as a commodity, arguing that if such money is backed up by gold, and since gold is a commodity, so also is money a commodity. This is flawed reasoning.

While money created by the central bank can be backed by any standard (numeraire), be it gold or other, it is not a means of selling (exchanging) that standard. Rather, such a monetary standard simply gives a stable currency value to money in circulation in goods and services that are transacted in markets according to their prices. It is the prices of goods and services that are stabilized by the choice of the monetary standard, and no exchange of the monetary numeraire has taken place.

Supply of money (also demand for money) as a concept pursuing commodity money means that money has a separate market, its exchange mechanism, and thereby, price for the commodity called money. This price of money is determined in the market for money. Textbooks treat the money matter this way; conventional banks honor money market transactions in this light. The concept of equilibrium quantities of money, output and interest rates is then determined.

Money supply and money demand are concepts used to extend the theory of market mechanism to the monetary sector and keep economic theory cohesive by this nicety. The result is forced intellectualism used for exacerbating the human ego for interest rates, while ignoring the social ills caused by the consequences.

Supply of money as exogenously created money is undertaken both by the central bank and the commercial bank. This is done through the fractional reserve requirements maintained by the monetary authority. Central banks exercise the monetary instruments of reserve ratio, prime rate of interest (discount rate), open market operations in buying and selling bonds and moral suasion to influence the stock of money in the economy. The decision on the stock of money supply to be held in the central bank is based on its outlook regarding economic stabilization, guided by economic policies using exchange rate and interest rate mechanisms. No social issues enter this kind of economic determination.

Economic stabilization assumes that efficient financial market and the real economy exist, and that would set a stable market rate of interest and output, against which stabilization program will be charted. Likewise, a stable relationship between exchange rate and interest rate movements is assumed. Both of these assumptions are the most fickle in nature. They have failed to be predictive in the face of volatile capital markets.

Consequently, to determine the targets of fractional reserve requirements instruments on the basis of these mechanisms is most unreasonable. There cannot thereby be a match between the demand for and the supply of money in such erroneous estimations. There is no attempt on the part of the monetary authority to bridge this gap. Money is thereby created or contracted by the central bank by a persistence of this demand-supply gap. Hence, there remains a supply or demand concerning "money created as paper".

Commercial banks independently create a large supply of money out of their excess reserves. Excess reserves of commercial banks are deposited in the central bank as loanable funds after a statutory reserve is determined. Now, interbank borrowing brings about continuous interbank lending of the excess reserve at given rates of interest charged between banks.

The amount of credit creation now equals the huge amount created as follows: a one unit of currency (1) circulated over infinite number of rounds across interbank lending will generate new money to the tune of $1/r$, r being the statutory reserve ratio of the central bank.

Hence, if the reserve ratio is 10%, the amount of new money created equals 10 units of new money. The interest collected at 10% on extended interbank lending is, say, 1.10^n, for n finite rounds of relending. For $n = 10$, the interest collected is 25.94 financial units. The total amount of new money created is approximately 35.94 financial units. If the same process is carried on by m number of banks, say $m = 100$, the total new money and the interest income on it at 10% yields New Money = 3,594 financial units. Allowing for some productive capacity in the economy attained through interbank lending in accordance with the money-real economy tradeoff we have discussed above, the interbank lending would have created a substantial part of the 3,594 money units as new money in the economy. This new money caused by multiple credit creation net of productive use, if any, is the "money created as paper". This amount of money is the potential withdrawal from productive capacity in the good things of life. All the previous arguments against this kind of unproductive creation of money can be recalled here.

9.1.3 *Quantity theory of money*

Quantity theory of money does not accept the concepts of supply and demand for money. Money is in proportion to how effectively it is mobilized. Thus, the quantity of money is a proportion of the need for money. The equation of exchange in quantity theory of money is,

$$M.V = P.Y \qquad (9.1)$$

This is alternatively written as

$$M = (1/V).P.Y = k.T \qquad (9.2)$$

M denotes the quantity of money; V denotes the velocity of money circulation; P denotes price level; Y denotes real output; $P.Y$ denotes the total value of transactions; $k = (1/V)$. In the limiting case when all of the financial resource is mobilized, then this k is equivalent to having one full unit of monetary stock injected into the economy (as aggregate transaction) 100%. Then, $v = 1$ (though this assumption is not restrictive) and $M = T$.

A generalized equation of exchange (Friedman, 1989) qualifies T in terms of the dual sectors and their prices and yields. These comprise the financial sector with value of savings in securities $(l_1, l_2, \ldots, l_n)$ and the term structure of interest rates in this portfolio, denoted by $(i_1, i_2, \ldots, i_n)$. Hence, $T = T(l_1, l_2, \ldots, l_n, i_1, i_2, \ldots, i_n, Y)$. M now pursues all such assets and thus gets subjected to the same kinds of problems as were found to exist in the case of the fractional reserve requirements monetary system. Besides, the convergence to the limiting case of $v = 1$ (i.e., considering the whole spending in one round) involves a transformation from the fractional reserve requirements monetary system to a 100% Reserve Requirements Monetary System (RRMS). Thereby, a lot of institutional restructuring, monetary numeraire selection (gold and silver = bimetallic), changes in policy instruments, and readiness on the part of the public domain and global relations are needed.

In the further case of independence by competition between the financial sector and the real economy, the equation of exchange can be written as

$$M = T_1(l_1, l_2, \ldots, l_n, i_1, i_2, \ldots, i_n) \times T_2(Y) = A.M_1 \times M_2 \qquad (9.3)$$

Here, M_1 and M_2 are specific quantities of money in the two competing sectors. It is obvious now that under an optimal quantity of money M (according to quantity theory), the two quantities M_1 and M_2 move oppositely. A is a proportion of the quantity of money in circulation. It is a function of the velocities of money circulation in the two sectors. Such velocities as functions of all the other variables in the two sectors are oppositely related. Thereby, all the trappings of monetary mechanism in the presence of money-real economy tradeoff are introduced in the quantity theory of money, as in the case of the Keynesian monetary theory, which was explained earlier. This kind of dichotomy is both an impossibility in and a barrier to a transformation into 100% RRMS. The quantity theory of money as stated in terms of expression (9.3) thus repeats the creation of paper money.

9.1.4   *Functions of money*

The concepts of demand and supply of money and the interest-bearing equation of exchange in quantity theory of money are untenable as they play their role in the unproductive function of creating "money created as paper". Thereby, the notions regarding the functions of money must also be reconsidered. This issue is not simply a conceptual one. It has a deep impact on the understanding of the relationships between money, real economy, markets and asset valuation.

None of these functions of money is tenable in the Universal Paradigm project on economy, money and finance. The exchange value of money and its store of value lose meaning. Only the monetary function as a unit of valuation is retained. Why?

Exchange value of money assumes that future markets for goods exist either in complete or incomplete form. This is never true, because of lack of full information and the presence of uncertainty. Hence, there cannot be a matching amount of money to do the function in such projected markets, for which a future demand and supply and a quantity of money is allowed to flow in today. This argument also brings to an end the notion of the time-value of money, which can exist only in relation to a future function of money in terms of its exchange value, and this is indeterminate.

The function of money as a store of value is rejected, because money has no intrinsic value of its own. It is valued as a quantity of money in the 100% RRMS by relating money and finance to the real economy. Even in the case of the gold standard (or bimetallic), this case by itself does not establish the 100% RRMS, if resources are not fully mobilized in life-sustainable goods and services. Hence, the store of value is to be found truly in the real economy, and it is determined by prices of real goods and services that relate to ethicizing market exchange. This topic was examined earlier. The real economy thereafter reveals the real growth rate of output of life-sustaining goods and services. Money as currency becomes valuable or is devalued according to the productivity so transferred to it by the real economy.

Only money as unit of valuation applies in the 100% RRMS interconnecting $M1$ and $M2$ and all the inhering variables by complementary relations. Money as the unit of valuation measures the value of the assets or goods that are transacted in ethicizing market exchange as they present themselves at a point in time and with the environing contingencies of the markets. This result is not automatic. It requires IIE-processes to prevail between the monetary sector, financial sector and the real economy. The intensity of such complementarities is estimated by means of the circular causation relations expressed through analytical expressions between the state and policy variables under the impact of knowledge flows and sequentially in respect of the selected endogenous variables.

The circular causation interrelations between the entities are formalized as follows in reference to the following simulation problem of money and the real economy:

$$\text{Simulate } M = T_1^a . T_2^b; \quad a + b > 1, \ a > 0, \ b > 0, \qquad (9.4)$$
$$\text{subject to } T_1 = f_1(T_2) \,; T_2 = f_2(T_1),$$

recursively by circular causation relations
between the variables.

T_1 and T_2 are expressed in terms of the variables of these transaction functions. Recursive circular causation interrelations exist between these variables.

Now, the financial and real economy sectors are complemented by the rate of return on real assets and by prices representing values of ethical market exchange. Spending in the real economy means that there are interconnecting financial instruments in the financial sector that mobilize financial resources in the direction of productive spending on the good things of life. The two transactions are simultaneous, and thereby, complementary. They interact by circular causation relations between them in terms of their recursively determined state and policy variables.

9.2   Returning to the E-O-O-E Model for Explaining the Money, Finance and Real Economy Complementarities

Some of the underlying issues have already been introduced previously. The important remaining issues are on the nature of money and how the 100% RRMS will work. No detailed discussion is taken up here. For details, see Choudhury and Hoque (2004).

To compare the two processes of generating money in relation to commodities, we note firstly the Money-Commodification-Money (MCM) relationship (Heilbroner, 1985; Carchedi, 1991). In this model, money is treated as a commodity and is used to assign values to market commodities. Consequently, the relationship points to the exogenous intrinsic value of money that finds an independent market, the money market. Thereby, the money prices of market commodities reflect the effect of the supply or quantity of money in the economy on prices caused by spending. This relationship from the side of money to market commodities and economic output is considered to generate price pressure. Hence, increased amounts of money lead to higher spending, upward price pressure, and thereby, more money to finance the on-going inflationary regime of spending and prices. Nominal interest rates increase with inflationary trend.

When seen from the Marxist point of view, the political economy implications are used to argue that monetary controls are done by powerful and rich financiers, private owners and governments in favor of the former ones. The culture of money lending at higher rates of interest comes to their benefit. Such monies appear in the form of risky portfolios and output. These outputs move in conflicting dynamics, as was explained earlier. Consequently, the commodification of money comes about by the continued control over money matters. Savings, interest rates and debt financing become endemic in this kind of monetary deal. Subsequently, the higher power needed to perpetuate the cycle of financial power and speculative financing brings about more money creation in response to the kind of commodification that is generated by self-interest. Money thus loses its social function. It remains as a stock under capitalist control reinforcing the capitalist continuing power.

Next, consider the E-O-O-E model for the money-finance-real economy interrelations. In this case, money is a social contravention and instrument for bringing about just, equitable and sustainable improvement in human well-being. Economic relations are taken up within the full gamut of social considerations and forces. M now belongs to a category of primary goods in accordance with the divine law that delineates the basis of the ethicizing social, economic and financial relations.

The underlying well-being function can be selected variously. Let us consider the well-being function and the circular causation between variables for purposes of simulating the quantity of money in tandem with the demand for real goods and services. One such form of the simulation problem under money, finance and real economy appears in expression (9.4).

The E-O-O-E money, finance and real economy model can now be written down:

The concept of M as spiritual good appears in the divine text. Thus, $M \in (\Omega, S)$. Since the knowledge explaining M is also explained in the divine text (e.g., Qur'an and the Sunnah), such references become the divine rule governing money. We therefore have $\theta \in (\Omega, S)$. Now, $Z(\theta) = (\theta, M(\theta))$ becomes a theme found in the Moral Law. The principle of $Z(\theta)$ under the moral law is next subjected to discourse for further understanding the complementarities (i.e., pairing in the Qur'an) of money with all the good things of life (likewise, inverse of bad = good, e.g., since interest rate i is "bad", the good is $1/i$).

Thereafter, the epistemic origin of $Z(\theta)$ leads to the ontological conceptualization of the moral law under which it is to be understood as a complementary relational entity designed to arise from and thereafter perpetuate the unity of the entities. At this stage, $Z(\theta)$ is further extended by market variables, financial instruments, policy instruments and institutional arrangements (denoted by $X(\theta)$) to perpetuate the $Z(\theta)$ relationship under the moral law in this broadly embedded spectrum of unifying complementary interrelationships.

Finally, the ontic evaluation of the well-being function, as in expression (9.4), is carried out and improvements conducted to evolve the money, finance and real economy relations by circular causation between the state and policy variables related to the above sectors.

The contrast between the MCM and the E-O-O-E model on money, finance and real economy, though procedurally similar, are yet substantively different. This fact is shown in Figure 9.1.

Though both processes of money creation are endogenous, the MCM model is not a learning model by virtue of its lack of learning in unity of knowledge. The principal structure of the endogenous relationship between money, finance and real economy is based on the replacement of interest-bearing business by trade. Trade is further complemented with spending in charity in the broadest sense of this word, encompassing all of human well-being, importantly, justice and poverty alleviation. For the complementary linkages to occur,

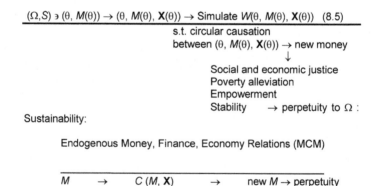

$$(\Omega, S) \ni (\theta, M(\theta)) \rightarrow (\theta, M(\theta), X(\theta)) \rightarrow \text{Simulate } W(\theta, M(\theta), X(\theta)) \quad (8.5)$$

s.t. circular causation
between $(\theta, M(\theta), X(\theta)) \rightarrow$ new money
$\downarrow$

Social and economic justice
Poverty alleviation
Empowerment
Stability $\rightarrow$ perpetuity to Ω :

Sustainability:

Endogenous Money, Finance, Economy Relations (MCM)

$M \quad \rightarrow \quad C\,(M, X) \quad \rightarrow \quad$ new $M \rightarrow$ perpetuity

Figure 9.1: Endogenous Money, Finance and Real Economy Relations by IIE-Processes

the establishment of 100% RRMS with the gold standard becomes mandatory.

Now, the relationship between the central bank, the commercial bank and the economy is by virtue of the IIE-process dynamics jointly determined and shared between these domains. The central bank looks wholly after economic stabilization and protects the currency in circulation as resource by means of gold or bimetallic numeraire. The commercial bank is the financial intermediary for resource mobilization in partnership with its clientele through shareholding and stakeholding. The clientele, the commercial bank and the central bank maintain cooperative mechanisms to realize and perpetuate such a partnership. Knowledge formation on the premise of unity of knowledge as systemic integration is viewed to be central to this partnership. The E-O-O-E model thus presents the complementary structure of circular causation relations between institutional and socioeconomic actions and responses.

9.3   Conclusion

Money is a financial contravention having deep social relevance. It is fundamentally required to define ownership, responsible exercise of power, and a market process and exchange. All these generate the power of money in realizing justice, equality and poverty alleviation. Money of such a kind is endogenous in terms of the unifying complementary relations with the rest of the embedded system variables. The E-O-O-E model projects this kind of endogenous money, finance and real economy circular causation relations to simulate levels of social well-being.

Contrary to such a property of endogenous money are both of the following: firstly, there is exogenous money as "money created as paper". Secondly, money can be endogenous, starting first from an exogenous stock, and then, through the cycle of commodification of itself, money increases in volume independently of the real economy.

The question of money, finance and real economy interrelations by means of complementarities between them does appear in this endogenous money concept. In modern times, such endogenous money is the plastic card. It prevails due to an insatiable excess demand to hold money by individuals, households and firms. The result has been towering debt.

Under the regime of exogenous money and the latter type of endogenous money concept, there not being any complementarities between the good things of life (e.g., money, finance, poverty alleviation, justice, resource mobilization), there cannot also exist social well-being. The precise definition of money and its relationships in the total socio-scientific spectrum is therefore essential.

Money in the E-O-O-E model presents this other definition. Money is now defined as the value of spending in the good things of life. In the other monetary concepts, we have pointed out that the presence of the logic of demand, supply and interest-bearing quantity theory of money denies a precise definition of money in the social and economic sense taken together.

Chapter

10

The Illogical Basis of Interest Rates

10.1   A Philosophical Discourse Regarding the Rejection of Interest

The question asked here is whether interest is necessary as against whether it is moral. The moral question was not answered in the previous chapters. We now extend our argument to involve the moral question, with the question of rejection of interest on grounds of it being unnecessary. Our vantage point of the philosophical argument is that morality encompasses all aspects of life in a holistic way. This is unlike ethics, which, if it does not emanate from the moral law, can be simply humanistic in kind, and thereby, subject to the rationalist ego.

Incorporating the discussion on interest in the frame of the moral law must look at its rejection from the argumentative premise that if a social act and response is unnecessary, such an act is unacceptable. There is no conditionality of this fact, for the moral law is not time and space bound. It is universal over continuums of knowledge-induced space and time dimensions. It establishes the Universal Paradigm as the worldview. On the other hand, if the moral law sanctions an act or response, then such an act and response cannot be logical. The moral law is established on the most irreducible premise of the penultimate truth. This is the irreducibility axiom that is proven by the analytical method known as self-referencing, not imposed in our thought and the issues, problems and systems under investigation.

Briefly, this means that only the irreducible element that can explain the whole universe completely and uniquely is worthy of being referred to all the time in the process of analysis and thought. We call this irreducible element the fundamental epistemology of Oneness of God as it is explicated in the divine law as the moral law. In the Qur'an, the Oneness of God, as it is intrinsic to the moral or the divine law, is recalled continuously and over continuums of issues. We have referred to this as "recalling" at every point along the evolutionary dynamics of the E-O-O-E model.

The following schematic argumentation can establish the fact that *Riba*/interest is both morally unacceptable and unnecessary. Consider Figure 10.1, which is self-explanatory. The middle box establishes the

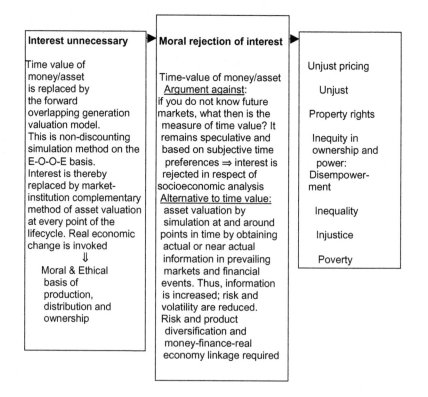

Figure 10.1:   Moral Rejection and Unnecessary Nature of *Riba*/Interest

claim that interest is morally reprehensible (right-hand side) and it is unnecessary (left-hand side).

Thus, define the moral law by

$$\text{Moral Law} = M(\theta^*, \mathbf{X}^*(\theta^*); \wp).$$

Here, $\mathbf{X}^*(\theta^*) = \{R$, money, finance, real economy variables, policy measures and financing instruments replacing interest$\}$.

The simulation of well-being criterion subject to circular causation relations between the $(\theta^*, \mathbf{X}^*(\theta^*); \wp)$-variables applies in reference to the E-O-O-E model of the worldview methodology along the IIE learning paths.

10.2   Irrational Exuberance of Interest Financing

Myopic foresight causes individuals to be carried away by interest-rate financing and interest-based instruments. The argument individuals make in favor of interest-banking is that this pays them risk-free and inflation-correcting returns at any point in time. Yet, if we note the popularity of Islamic Bank Bangladesh's interest-free deposits, for instance, this is phenomenal. The large *number* of deposits — a mix of small and large denominations in volumes, coming mostly from ordinary people in everyday walks of life — has made this bank enjoy the highest deposit rate of all commercial banks in Bangladesh. This success has been repeated over several years now. This pattern of deposits has made Islamic Bank Bangladesh an exemplary one among Islamic banks internationally.

We can read a number of individual traits of depositors in relation to the banking function (Choudhury and Hussain, 2005). Individuals clearly do not exhibit the type of risk-averse behavior as interest-prone depositors. That is because the Islamic mode of financing has the endogenous money-real economy relationships that effectively diversify risk by increasing production in diverse outlets and increasing the number of shareholders.

We have mentioned above that the compound effect of production diversification and risk diversification with increasing number of shareholders (depositors) progressively reduces unit risk sharply, both in the idiosyncratic and systemic sense. One of the injunctions of the Shari'ah (Islamic Law) is protection of property rights. In the case of bank deposits, this injunction is satisfied by progressive reduction of total risk of shareholding. This of course does not mean that risk will be run down to zero. Yet, the cooperative financing instruments of profit and loss sharing, trade financing and secondary financing instruments that revolve around the primary ones, are enhanced by continuously sharing the total risk.

The success of deposits in interest-free shares is increasingly proving itself in many Islamic and non-Islamic banking outlets. In Malaysia, Indonesia and Pakistan, interest-bearing banks are well-known to have opened up dual windows for the promotion of their businesses to Islamic-prone depositors. Islamic and financing businesses are prospering worldwide today. In Sudan, Islamic bank is not simply universally accepted, but also the Islamic principles of money, finance and real economic developments are becoming ingredients of policy-making (Ibrahim, 2005).

10.3   Flaws in Mainstream Financial Theory

The above indications in depositors' behavior show that in order to ground depositors' preferences on risk aversion, the variance of returns from portfolios of investment must be understood separately from risk aversion in securities. It is the learning parameter in the interest-free case, which by bringing about risk diversification and product diversification through the money, finance and real economy linkages, causes the propensity on the depositors to enter shareholding with Islamic financial intermediaries.

Once the risk diversification gains momentum and attains long-term sustainability, the service charges that are initially required to pay for operating shares is reduced. This comes about not simply by the same formula of risk diversification. Rather, by expanding production and inter-entity linkages (sectors, joint production, community, inter-institutional, trade, etc.), more outlets for profitability of operations are opened up. Service charges in Islamic Bank Bangladesh is much lower than in interest-driven banks. Depositors can open accounts with a bare minimum of funds, so that the charges too remain low in maintaining such small denominations of funds from ordinary village depositors. Conventional banks require a minimum of Taka 10,000 to open up personal accounts in Bangladesh. Consequently, their service charges per account are much higher. Service charge is applied on the volume of deposits.

Now, returning to the risk aversion question, here are two ways that this is viewed. Individuals are wrongly made to believe in the one-dimensional preference behavior based on such a construction of the risk aversion measure. We have all felt alarmed on many occasions by the fear that travel agents and car rentals put on users to take out insurance. Yet, we know that adverse selection does not occur in most cases by not taking out such insurances. Risk by accidents follows a Poisson Probability Distribution, not a Normal Probability Distribution, on the frequency of accidents (Hogg and Craig, 1965).

10.3.1   *Risk aversion (mainstream finance)*

The mainstream finance view is to minimize the Variance ($\mathbf{X}$) while increasing Expected Value of $\mathbf{X}$ in the individual (household) utility function, which is assumed to be an objective criterion for individual and household decision-making on holding funds in alternative ways. The expected utility function in risk and return is given by $U = U(E(\mathbf{X}), \mathrm{Var}(\mathbf{X}))$. Risk aversion realized by maximizing $U(E(\mathbf{X}), \mathrm{Var}(\mathbf{X}))$, subject to household budget, yields $dE(\mathbf{X})/d\mathrm{Var}(\mathbf{X}) < 0$. Bold variable denotes vectors.

The question now is whether interest-bearing really causes the risk aversion indicator to be attained by way of risk diversification? Clearly, if interest rate is high and increasing, that is to finance risk. Thereby, $d\mathrm{Var}(\mathbf{X}) > 0$ under the impact of higher interest rates. The causation here is from the side of the existence of higher and increasing interest rates in increasingly risky regimes of financing. Yet, individual and households are made to heighten their preferences towards holding the so-called interest-bearing savings.

Therefore, $dE(\mathbf{X}) > 0$. Thereby, $dE(\mathbf{X})/d\mathrm{Var}(\mathbf{X}) > 0$. This is a contradiction between risk averse behavior and what risk aversion formula suggests. The problem is caused by the adverse selection effects of interest on risk and savers' knowledge.

10.3.2   *Risk aversion as risk diversification in the learning model of unity of knowledge*

Clearly, the above is not the case when endogenous relations between money, finance and real economy linkages diversify production and risk along with better household and business knowledge on financial decision-making. Linkages are measured by the systemic knowledge values (θ-values). Thereby, we come to redefine the indicators by the following symbols: $\mathrm{Var}(\theta, \mathbf{X}(\theta))$. Now, the usual relations hold: $d\mathrm{Var}(\theta, \mathbf{X}(\theta))/d\theta < 0$, while, $dE(\mathbf{X})/d\theta > 0$. Thereby, $dE(\mathbf{X})/d\mathrm{Var}(\mathbf{X}) < 0$.

Now, once again, the relationship between risk diversification, production diversification in a regime of increased linkages, learning and the subsequent lowering of interest rates, all lead to an increase in the real rate of return. Thereby, the above conditions hold true. At the same time, we also note that the optimality condition of risk-return utility behavior cannot hold in the case of $\mathbf{X}$-learning by θ-values. This can be readily shown, but its simple mathematics is not done here in respect of simulating the well-being criterion function, $W(\theta, E(\theta, \mathbf{X}(\theta)), \mathrm{Var}(\theta, \mathbf{X}(\theta)))$.

10.3.3   *Adverse relations of interest rates*

Much of the arguments raised in this section have been already covered before. Our intention here is to prove that interest-bearing relations generate circular causation between the variables affected by interest. This kind of compounded causality heightens the degree of total risk.

We have examined the following causality: interest rate i deepens savings, $S(i, y)$, with y as national output. Deepening savings cause financial resource withdrawal from the economy. Thereby, the pressure on debt financing ($D(i, y)$) by means of bonds and borrowing, $B(i, y)$, increases. Consequently, by compounding, we obtain $D(S(B(i, y)))$, denoting debt as the compound effect of the cumulative factors involving interest rate i.

Next, examine this compound case by reflexive causation: $D(i, y)$ causes debt financing by means of $B(i, y)$, which is caused by savings $S(i, y)$, which in turn is caused by i. Consequently, the economy moves in continuous cycles of gyration inwards, with y being locked in the sub-potential level of national output.

We now have two equivalent gyrations of risk (variance) relations, but with different amplitudes. Firstly, Var(D) equals a complex aggregation of variances and covariances between $S(i, y)$, $B(i, y)$ and i. Conversely, Var(i) equals a complex aggregation of variances and covariances of $D(i, y), S(i, y)$ and $B(i, y)$. In the same way, other complex circular causality can be generated between $S(i, y)$ and the other variables in respect of i and sub-optimal y; and of $B(i, y)$ with the other variables.

The conclusion from the above arguments is that holding and financing of interest-bearing assets only heightens the risk propensity of the economy as a whole and of its component businesses and sectors. This result goes against the irrational exuberance based on a flawed belief that interest rate protects property against risk.

10.4 The E-O-O-E Implications

Two facts are sufficient to point out here. First, the circular causality in the interest-related domain as explained by the above kinds of gyrations between economic and social variables is a result of the E-O-O-E model in respect of "de-knowledge" as opposed to knowledge. De-knowledge is the process of disintegration in the social aspects of unity of divine knowledge and all this maintains. As a consequence in the real world, now the entities and sectors of the economy de-link themselves by obstructing an otherwise much needed catalytic force. Interest rate causes these kinds of de-linking by holding back the flow of resources as they get channelled into savings, bonds, borrowing and debt, away from spending in the real economy in the good and productive things of life. The result of the de-linking is reflected in the perpetual movement of the economy along a sub-optimal path of national output.

The opposite gyrating circles of a progressive economy can be improvised in terms of real rates of return, the phasing out of savings, bonds and borrowing, and debt overhang. This happens by means of circular causation caused by linkages between the r shown below (rate of return) and the attainment of potential national output. The effects caused by product diversification and risk diversification can once again be invoked here to explain the dynamics of evolutionary learning between agents, variables and sectors of the socioeconomic system.

10.5   Circular Causality between the Interest-Driven Variables: Time-Value of Money is Untenable

The principle of pervasive complementarities replaces the neoclassical postulate of marginal rate of substitution. This principle thus destroys the entire neoclassical theory, and thereby, the mainstream economic reasoning based on scarcity, conflict and competition, all of which are the *raison d'etre* of the neoclassical postulate of marginalism. Consequently, a different method replaces neoclassical resource valuation methods. We now carry on with the critique of the received valuation method, which has persisted in Islamic economics and finance with misleading fervor.

Let D_0 denote dividend payment on bonds at time $t = 0$, and whose coupon-yield represents the rate of interest i. Let g_R denote the growth rate of dividends arising from real economic activity. Let g_F denote the growth rate of dividends arising from financial activity. These two sectors exist in competing duality with each other.

According to our argument revolving around the (r/i) and (i/r) discount rates for the sectors dominated by real economic and financial activities, respectively, the present values of cash flows are given by

$$PV = \int_0^\infty D_0 e^{-(i/r - g_F)} dt = D_0/(g_F - i/r) > 0, \quad \text{with } g_F > (i/r),$$

$$\text{i.e., } i < g_F/r, \quad (10.1)$$

in respect of cash flows arising from the financial economy.

Expression (10.1) yields the following result:

$$dPV/di > 0; \quad dPV/dr < 0 \quad (10.2)$$

$$PV = \int_0^\infty D_0 e^{-(r/i - g_R)} dt = D_0/(g_R - r/i) > 0, \quad \text{with } g_R > (r/i),$$

$$\text{i.e., } i > r/g_F \quad (10.3)$$

for cash flows arising from the real economy.

Expression (10.3) yields the result:

$$dPV/di < 0; \quad dPV/dr > 0. \tag{10.4}$$

Expressions (10.1) and (10.2) show the tradeoff between i and r in respect of resource allocation in the financial and real sector duality according to the postulate of marginal rate of substitution. This is yet another way of stating that in the neoclassical roots of macroeconomics, the financial sector and real sector remain competing rather than complementary. Thereby, such sectors have their own versions of prices and returns. Through the tradeoff between i and r, financial resources get withdrawn from the real sector into the financial sector and vice versa.

Both mainstream economists and Islamic economists with mainstream persuasion have for long now pursued and legitimized the use of the present-valuation of cash flow method, and thereby, of the concept of time-value of money. They have missed the understanding that the time valuation of money is simply the shadow price of interest rate.

In this regard, the argument runs as follows: time-value of money is the result of the postulate of marginal rate of substitution between the competing sectors of savings (i) and real economy (mobilization of resources through the financial sector continuously to generate profitability r).

Marginal rate of substitution is rejected forever in the Tawhidi worldview of unity of knowledge between the two sectors that learn continuously in the IIE-processes. Besides, money pursues real goods and services in Shari'ah compliant outlets with complementarities between them, reflecting the existence of systemic unity of knowledge. For the future, we are not sure under any circumstances about the existence of markets then, and of the level of demand and the nature of changing human preferences as learning proceeds continuously. In the Islamic economic and social transformation, such behavioral changes bring about unification between money and real goods and between the ethicizing goods and services. The saying of Prophet Muhammad is that the price of a fruit cannot be ascertained before it is borne; the price of a fish cannot be set before it is landed for sale.

Besides, the uncertainties of the future over preference change and continuous learning cannot be estimated as datum by probabilistically expected values. We surmise here that such probabilities would be Quantum Field Probabilities estimated for events to happen *around* certain convergent points rather than be *exactly attained* at that point. The representation here is of multiple possibilities covered in a fuzzy topological field with probabilistic neighborhoods. Such probabilities would be of the kinds that appeared to Heisenberg in his Uncertainty Principle (1958). The determination of the true nature of probabilities in complex fields of events had defied Keynes as he pondered over it all his life (O'Donnell, 1989).

Contrary to the present-valuation method and its prototypes such as the internal rate of return, and certainty equivalent and asset valuation of shareholders' wealth, the Tawhidi methodology of systemic unity between money and real economy presents an alternative valuation method. This is the valuation method by means of the overlapping generation model. In it, valuation of assets and returns is carried out by the moment-to-moment terminal valuation of a stream of cash flows appearing *"nearest"* to the point of their actual occurrence, that is, occurring in the neighborhood cover of the actual hidden point of expected convergence. The estimation of such moment-to-moment cash flows is carried out by two combined approaches.

Since an equilibrium point permanently remains as an *"expectational"* point that can be only approximated to but never actually attained in the continuously learning model, therefore, cash flows are expected values with probabilistic correction by a factor. In our case, this correction factor was shown by the $\varepsilon(\theta)$-value.

Here, θ denotes the consensual assignment of a sequence of discoursed knowledge flows in the IIE-process, along with abstraction of the ontology for understanding the dynamics of unity of knowledge for the particular problem at hand. The cash flows now yield the valuation of the probabilistic cash flows *"nearest"* to an expected point of valuation hidden inside the probabilistic neighborhood of the actual point of convergence. The second factor determining the probability measure of cash flows *"nearest"* to the point of valuation is the institutionally guided discourse mechanism in the midst of the emerging IIE-processes. Valuation is thus explicitly a combination of market process, moral guidance and enforcement according to the ethical rules of the Shari'ah.

10.6   Conclusion

In this chapter, we have shown that interest rates have intrinsic debilitating effects on the economy, society and human well-being. They cause instability in economic earnings, cash flows and resource use. Conversely, the avoidance of interest is both a necessary as well as a moral prerogative. We have established that interest is untenable either in its static or time-dependent case of discounting in the asset valuation model. There is always a negative relationship between efficiency, productivity and interest rate. Economic and social policies are always aimed at sustaining the economy along the path of stabilization and social well-being. Interest rates and interest-based businesses and policies are inept to attain these goals. Hence, sound government and academic mediums ought to study the critical restructuring of their economies.

The E-O-O-E model that we have formalized as the reflection of the universal worldview methodology is the sure way to create sustainability and well-being of all. Yet, this is not a sheer wishful idea. It is deeply analytical and practical in essence. It is the calling of this book and in this chapter that interest rate and its circular causation dynamics cause the continuance of sub-potential levels of national output through the medium of every compounding debilitating activity of resource withdrawal. That savings lead to growth of investments and output in the future is a flawed reasoning of economic theory. Savings and interest are irrational exuberances of household preferences, which are next injected into the business environment as well. These problems of economics and society have to be understood in order to get out of the illusory trap caused by interest rates and their economic consequences. The E-O-O-E model and its circular causation in the embedded economy involving the appropriate set of variables reflect this kind of better prospects for stability, progress and well-being.

Chapter

11

Questioning Modernity by the Tawhidi Worldview

11.1 Modernity According to the Precept of Divine Oneness: A Methodological Summary

The goals of modernity and the core of divine oneness as the Tawhidi unity of knowledge providing the epistemic centerpiece are inextricably intertwined by their reflexive learning relations. This implies endogenous relational epistemology between complementing systems and their entities made up of agents, artefacts, relations and variables. But such artefacts cannot integrate unless they are derived from the premise of unity of knowledge that charts the knowledge flows throughout, and consequently, unleash evolutionary learning by means of the dynamics of complementarities (circular causation). The principle of pervasive complementarities that underlies such dynamics is the sure sign of explaining unification of knowledge between systems, issues, entities, their variables and relations.

Such unification of knowledge between things cannot come about unless there is a most reduced epistemological premise upon which the Universal Paradigm, the worldview and its methodology are constructed. Thereafter, the conceptualization of the epistemological worldview leads to enabling ways and means of attaining the goal of unity of knowledge and the sustainability of well-being. These require appropriate laws, guidance, institutions, policies and programs that must complement with the systemic variables, which we refer to here as state variables. Thus, learning based on the epistemology of oneness comes about by the Principle of and observation on Pervasive Complementarities. These are complementarities between state variables and institutional variables, thereby generating complementarities between the preferences of agents in the discursive processes over all issues. Complementarities are generated also by sustaining the uniqueness and universality of the methodology. The methodological model was derived and established by the phenomenological model of E-O-O-E.

In the first place, divine oneness appears as the fundamental epistemology. The precept of oneness is explained by the divine text of the Qur'an and the authentic Sunnah, and their guidance by inalienable rules and instruments that carry the derived ideas into application and continuity over everything (continuums). This universe of "everything" is particularized in this book to compromise the socio-scientific order.

The precept of oneness and the law governing it are axiomatically given as complete, absolute and perfect. The secondary laws, rules, guidance and instruments derived from the principal law of divine oneness and upon which details are discoursed by ways and means pronounced by the unity of the divine law (i.e., Shuratic processes), are perpetually in the state of cumulative evolutionary learning. Knowledge thus becomes the cause and effect of the evolutionary learning worldview in reference to the epistemology of oneness. Life, thought and experience are thereby organized and evolved according to the emanating directions of the relational epistemology premised on divine oneness and driven by its evolutionary dynamics.

We have already explained the formalism of the Tawhidi unity of life as the Universal Paradigm, the worldview having its distinctive methodology. We will not repeat those parts here. Our objective now is to integrate the various characteristics of modernity by and in the worldview of unity of knowledge. We thereby invoke the

E-O-O-E model for this purpose. Finally, we will examine whether the same kind of systemic integration is possible in any other paradigm. In essence, we are at the same time asking the question: does the principle of pervasive complementarities as the explanatory basis of unification of all possibilities exist in any paradigm other than the Tawhidi worldview? Likewise, it is also to raise the question whether the instruments underlying the E-O-O-E methodology can be found in any other doctrinaire.

11.1.1   *The dynamics of modernity according to the law of divine oneness*

One may wonder why we have taken to the use of the word "oneness" in general this time, and not to our earlier usage of the term, Tawhidi unity of knowledge. The meanings of all these terms are equivalent. We choose to use the term "oneness" in the generalized sense to convey the meaning that the divine law reflects unity of knowledge in "everything".

This is a scientific question that can be explained by the theory of neuro-cybernetics applied to study the episteme of unity of knowledge. The systemic variables and entities learn intrinsically by means of unity of knowledge as the inherent episteme of such a system. The human mind and observation explain this unity of systemic knowledge. In doing so, the human world establishes the appropriate institution and instruments of discourse and guidance. So *oneness* means intrinsic unity of knowledge axiomatically caused by the Oneness of God in the scheme of all things — "everything".

We now show the realization of unity of knowledge between divine oneness and modernity by the IIE-process methodology of the E-O-O-E model. This is represented in Figure 11.1.

In Figure 11.1, we have made some simplifications. The following variables are selected and within some of them, as indicated, other variables are encapsulated. For instance, we select the variables FM = Free Market, which encapsulates in it productive private capital ownership; ENV = Environment, which encapsulates environment projects; MRE = Money and Real Economy, which encapsulates interest-free instruments; STAB = Stabilization, which encapsulates inflation control; ESJ = Economic and Social Justice. Participation is

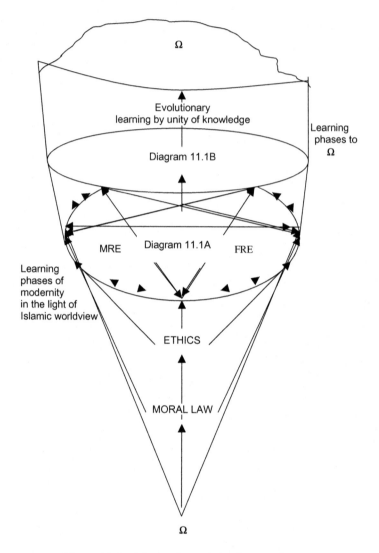

Figure 11.1:   Modernity and the Oneness Precept

indicated by double arrow causality under the meaning of circular causation or complementarities. Ethics is derived from the Moral Law, hence from the Tawhidi epistemology (Ω). Now we have the tuples of knowledge-induced vector along with knowledge flows, $\{(\theta, \mathbf{X}(\theta))\}$, where θ denotes the ethical base and is here implied by the complementarities generated by circular causations between the variables.

$\mathbf{X}(\theta) = (\text{FM, ENV, MRE, STAB, ESJ})$. The bracket {.} indicates the evolutionary learning tuples of this vector over phases of the IIE-learning processes in E-O-O-E model, as the understanding of the divine law in the human world increases, and thereby, takes hold over the evolving systems and their variables. Evolution by learning under the meaning of ethics derived strictly from the Moral Law premised on divine oneness (Ω) is shown by evolving conical circles. All IIE-processes emanate from the Ω-root and evolve cumulatively towards Ω again in the very large-scale universe. The Qur'an refers to this complete phenomenology of "everything" as the completion of learning across "everything" by Ω returning to Ω through the learning processes of all world-systems. This is the substantive meaning of the concept of "everything".

We display the whole Figure 11.1 in two integral parts. Diagram 11.1A displays the endogenous interrelationships between the above-mentioned variables. Diagram 11.1B integrates Diagram 11.1A into the phases of evolutionary learning according to the epistemology of divine oneness (Ω). Note that within Diagrams 11.1A and 11.1B, Ethics is shown to be strictly derived from the Moral Law. It then becomes the driving force for evolutionary learning. If this is not so, the other concept of Ethics would be based on sheer humanism. Humanism is a precept derived from rationalism. Rationalism rejects the moral premise and leaves all ethical determinations to human caprices as the primal cause of all causation. Contrarily, all evolutionary learning regarding unity of knowledge starts from and converges to Ω.

Well-being is a simulative objective criterion. It measures the attained levels of systemic unity of knowledge gained between the components of $\{(\theta, \mathbf{X}(\theta))\}$ and evaluated by circular causation between the complementary variables. This is followed by the reorganization of fresh paths of learning to gain the complementarities. Circular causation is implied by double-sided arrows. Evolution is shown by upward rising arrows.

Modernity according to the precept of unity of knowledge is depicted in Figure 11.1 in terms of evolutionary learning by complementarities in the $\{(\theta, \mathbf{X}(\theta))\}$-tuple vectors across phases of learning. Each phase is a continuous emanation from the previous one. This is similar to the concept of modernity given by Anthony Giddens (1983a) in respect of his theory of "presencing". It implies that modernity is the cause and effect of continuous movement by innovations and evolution.

Such a continuous version of knowledge-induced movements of $\{\theta, \mathbf{X}(\theta)\}$, in which is also taken up technological change as a specific variable with $\mathbf{X}(\theta)$, is depicted in Figure 11.2. Each circle gyrates upwards, starting from Ω and culminating in Ω again in the very large-scale universe (viz. *Akhira* = the Hereafter). The underlying dynamics

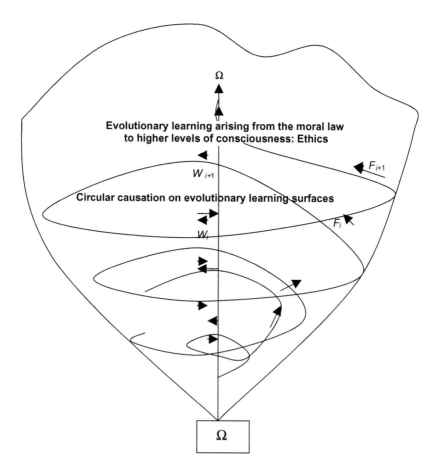

Figure 11.2:   Continuous Learning Version of Figure 11.1

here represent phases of circular causation relations and evolutionary learning as shown in Figure 11.1.

11.1.2   *Learning stages and circular causation*

Figure 11.2 further shows the evolutionary learning stages formed by circular causation between the evolutionary vector tuples, $(\{\theta\}, \{\mathbf{X}(\{\theta\})\})$. Subsequently, at the end of each of the corresponding IIE-processes, appears the simulation of well-being criterion function, given the circular causation equations (as in Figure 11.1).

It can then be shown that evolutionary circular causation relations F_i and F_{i+1} are related by $F_i \circ F_{i+1} = I$. Simulated well-being functions W_i and W_{i+1}, seen as relational mappings along the evolution of comprehension of ethics emanating from the moral law, are related by $W_i \circ W_{i+1} = i$. $i = 1, 2, \ldots$. And i denotes the identity mapping, so that each of the mappings, F_i and F_{i+1} and W_i and W_{i+1}, is inverse of another. This means that there are isomorphic mappings between these functionals. But for reasons of imperfection of knowledge, it is possible that statistical relations could exist. This condition of imperfection of knowledge flows at any stage of the IIE-processes would replace I by a function of θ-value limiting towards I. Say this statistical factor is $I + \varepsilon(\theta)$.

11.1.3   *Contrasting idea of modernity under the ethics of rationalism and its consequences on the evolutionary variables*

Figure 11.1 can be used to explain the evolutionary nature of modernity and capital accumulation as described by Schumpeter (1961), Hegel (1956), Marx (1969), Heilbroner (1985), Giddens (1983a) and others. The conjectural universe of Popper (1972) can be fitted in the same Figure 11.1. But all these will be a procedural exercise. Substantively, the two cases of modernity attained distinctly by oneness and rationalism are opposite to each other in meaning, spirit, content and organization.

In the case of a rationalistic definition of modernity, the moral law falls apart. Now, there is neither a beginning Ω nor the terminal Ω towards which the be-all and the end-all of existence inexorably converges. Rationalistic forms of individuated perceptions connected by an overdetermination of competing epistemologies emerge and define competing range of θ'-values. Consequently, the $\mathbf{X}'(\theta')$-values induced by θ'-devalues also become competing and unstable variables. Each $\{\theta', \mathbf{X}'(\theta')\}$ is now a socially differentiated value.

In the same way, by a continuation of this argument, each component of this $\{\theta', \mathbf{X}'(\theta')\}$-tuple becomes conflicting and competing between themselves. Thereby, the double arrow indicating causality implies weakening up into inward gyrating causality. Finally, the integrity of the cone in Figure 11.1 crumbles. Modernity now gets explained by the ever competing and conflicting rise of the domains of human activities based on ego. This was explained earlier in respect of the nature of methodological individualism.

11.2   Conclusion

In this chapter, we have extended the implications of the avoidance of interest to new levels incorporating philosophical and further economic arguments. Under no circumstances can interest be a tenable charge. Even the idea of attaining modernity by means of interest-based financing, businesses and human exuberant preferences, leads to an untenable idea. All these interest-based approaches are to be replaced by participatory socioeconomic instruments.

We have argued that sound economic and social policies must look at the phasing out of interest rates and their replacement by participatory development financing instruments. We have shown that such participatory instruments can increase the well-being of individuals and communities through greater degrees of stability, sustainability, wealth and development. In explaining all these, we have used the contrasting viewpoints, the E-O-O-E model of unity of knowledge and the interest-based financing regimes of mainstream economic and social worlds. In this area of investigation, the issue of modernity in the light of the episteme of unity of knowledge, which we referred to here as the universal oneness, was discussed.

Chapter

12

Conclusion

The worldview of the Universal Paradigm is a revolutionary challenge to mainstream economic, social, ethical and scientific doctrines that have filled up the pages and swayed the Western mind for the last two hundred years and more. The fact is that Western civilization, despite its great technological and scientific feats, has increasingly proved to be bereft of morals and ethics. The Occidental world-system neither has the methodology nor the will and mind to *endogenize* the true meaning of ethics, participation and unity in the comity of self and other. This is true as much of the body of academic intellection as for the practitioner's world, for the individual and the community.

The challenge that the Universal Paradigm presents in terms of its new world-systems, including its conceptions and applications, institutions and sustainable future, is the premise of oneness of the divine law, which in the Qur'an is referred to as *Tawhid*. The epistemology, ontology and applications of the Tawhidi worldview, equivalent with the Universal Paradigm, is the functional nature of unity of knowledge between systems and their relations and entities. This epistemic groundwork of reality is enabled by Islam.

Contrary to the occidental fact, this book has shown that an equivalent worldview to formalize and apply to issues of science and society, including economics and ethics, with the force of logical formalism, is non-existent in any doctrine other than the worldview of unity of knowledge. Hence, this book has brought out the Universal Paradigm of unity of the divine law, equivalently established by the Qur'anic Tawhidi worldview as the unique way for substantively examining, formalizing and realizing deep access in the study of reality in all world-systems. The emergent concepts of universality and uniqueness in this book have been referred to in this book as the learning domain of "everything".

In this expanding domain induced by the episteme of unity of knowledge premised on the divine law, all issues assume their concrescent forms and explanations. Thereby, the numinous emptiness of the meaning of cosmic interconnectedness is replaced by the ontological and applied aspects of the particular, the specific and the extensive. Within such exact forms of relations, meanings, explanations, verifications and inferences assume functional and logical forms.

This book has brought this nature of the epistemological study of the divine law of Oneness of God in the perspective of some of those issues that matter to economics, society, science, morals and ethics in everyday mundane life. The new worldview as against the temporary scientific revolution *a la* Kuhn, Kant and the eighteenth-century Enlightenment, was explained and applied to specific problems of money, financial interest, economic change, environmental sustainability, institutionalism and theory and practice. The book has thus carried on the legacy of the great works that since long ago have pursued the incessant project of unity of knowledge in the order of reality.

The futuristic view of the idea presented in this book is a new way for examining post-modern thought. From the beginning, the question posed is whether post-modernity will be any different from the occidental world-system of today's modernity. The arguments in this book simply project a post-modernist continuation of the permanent character of individualism and competition as opposed to participation; of capitalism and socialism as opposed to holistic well-being under the principle of pervasive complementarities between all entities of the system called "everything". Consequently, post-modernity is nothing but the old occidental paradigm in a new guise of argumentation as conflict and social Darwinism persist on in it.

Contrary to such a view of a fragmented human, a grand ecological future under post-modernity is the absolutely inverted worldview of unity of knowledge. The arguments of this book point out that across the great divide in the human threshold of tomorrow, the rise of Islam is as true as it is natural and permanent. Islam erases the coloring of the human future away from godless materialism into divine consciousness under unity of the divine law. The arguments of this book have brought out the fact that only Islam can deliver this new worldview beyond the narrow precincts of scientific revolution, yet with its impermanence. The Islamic world-system equipped with this kind of the fundamental worldview is already presenting itself and will intensify into a new framework of the human future with its Social Well-Being Criterion. The consequences will be pervasive. Such consequences will alter the old paradigms of thought and applications to create the new, even as this momentum has been unleashed.

The epistemological model of the Islamic worldview premised on unity of the divine law comprises the Qur'an and the prophetic moral guidance in "everything". Such is the permanent, unique and thus universal and unique gift to all the worlds. While the vistas of new thought remain a challenge to people of goodwill everywhere, they also erect the cherished goal of civilization to work towards them. This is in the least a scientific praxis for everyone and "everything", if not a religious belief that may not necessarily be embraced by everyone. Truth, tolerance and meaningful discourse are some of the attributes of discharging our duties as citizens of the planet earth and its future.

Glossary of Arabic Terms

Akhira   The Hereafter

Alameen   World-systems of the Qur'an

Allah   The One, True and Irresistible God as Creator and Sustainer of all.
              The Qur'an (Qur'an, 112:1–4) declares:
              "Say He is Allah, the One and Only, Allah the Eternal, Absolute; He begets not, nor is He begotten; and there is none like unto Him."

Ayath   Meant both as verses of the Qur'an and as evidences of recognition of the Oneness of God

Dhururiyath Basic needs, essentials

Fitra   Essence of goodness in things caused by the implementation of the divine law

Hajiyath   Comforts of life

Ibadah   Worship of the One true God without any material configuration in shape and form or by implication

Ijma   Social consensus following discourse on matters or established by the Qur'an and Sunnah (see below) as unequivocal for the Muslim community

Ijtihad   Search for truth on grounds of the fundamental source of the Qur'an, Sunnah and further discourse, using these to derive rules for life on specific issues

Israf   Wastage caused by the profligate

Lauh Mahfuz	The mother of the book, Al-Qur'an, mentioned in the Qur'an as the primordial Qur'anic text resting with God Almighty until the Judgement Day when it will be revealed to all
Qur'an	The last of the revealed books revered by Muslims as the true world of God and expression of the divine law
Riba	Interest and usury of any magnitude as excess over a due claim both in financial (*Riba al-Fadl*) and fungible forms (*Riba al-Nasia*)
Shari'ah	Islamic Law enacted by the epistemological sources of the Qur'an and the Sunnah and the secondary practice of discourse among the learneds who derive rules from the foundational sources
Shura	Consultative body in Islam, used in this book to mean also the grand participatory process of interactive and consensual learning between diverse entities, as conveyed by the Qur'an
Shuratic process	The process of participation, consultation leading to interaction, integration and creative evolution of knowledge in respect of all discursive matters under investigation
Sunnah	Practices and sayings of the Prophet Muhammad explicating the Qur'anic exegesis on all issues of life
Tahsaniyath	Refinements of life
Tasbih	Submission to God in utter humility and recognition of the Signs of oneness of the divine law
Tawhid	Oneness of God, oneness of the divine law (hence also Tawhidi). *Tawhid* also means "unicity" of the divine law explaining complementarities in and between "everything"

Zakat   Islamic tax on wealth and savings for meeting social needs of which there are eight categories. The categories, along with their possible extensions, are as follows: establishment of the rule of Allah (*Tawhid*) in all possible ways including wars by the Islamic state, meeting the basic needs for the needy, meting out debts for the needy, welfare for the kith and kin, for the wayfarer in the way of spreading the message of Islam, for orphans, new and needy Muslims, and salaries of those who administer the *Zakat* fund (Qur'an, 2:117, 9:60)

References

Alam, M.N. (2006), "The influences of 'societal sector institutions' in promoting lender-borrower network relationships between Islamic banks and cottage industry owners", *Humanomics*, 22:2, 67–83.

Aquinas, T. (1946), "The existence of God in things", "The infinity of God", "The eternity of God", "The unity of God", "Of God's knowledge", in *Summa Theologiae*, Vol. 1, pp. 1–11, 30–34, 40–45, 46–48, 72–86. New York, NY: Benziger Brothers, Inc.

Arrow, K.J. (1974), *The Limits of Organization*. New York, NY: W.W. Norton.

Azid, T. (2001), "Moving equilibrium model in an Islamic economy and its implications on Islamic Common Market", Paper presented at the International Conference on Economic Theory and Structural Change, University Utara Malaysia, Sintok, Malaysia.

Barker, E. (1999), *The Political Thought of Plato and Aristotle*. New York: Dover Publications.

Barrow, J.D. (1991), *Theories of Everything: The Quest for Ultimate Explanation*. Oxford, UK: Oxford University Press.

Blaug, M. (1968), *Economic Theory in Retrospect*, Homewood, IL: Richard D. Irwin.

Bohm-Bawerk, E. von. (1890), *Capital and Interest*. London, England: William Smart.

Boland, L.A. (1991), "On the methodology of economic model building", in *The Methodology of Economic Model Building*, pp. 39–63. London, England: Routledge.

Carchedi, G. (1991), *Frontiers of Political Economy*. New York, NY: Verso.

Carnap, R. (1966), "Kant's synthetic *a priori*", in M. Gardner (ed.), *Philosophical Foundations of Physics*. New York: Basic Books, Inc.

Choudhury, M.A.

(1989), *Islamic Economic Co-operation*. London, England: Macmillan Press Ltd.

(1990), "Islamic development cooperation: Issues and problems", *Journal of Economic Cooperation Among Islamic Countries*, 11:4.

(1992), *The Principles of Islamic Political Economy: A Methodological Inquiry*. London, England: Macmillan.

(1993), *Islamic Socio-Scientific Order and World System*. Universiti Sains Malaysia, Penang: Secretariat of Islamic Philosophy and Science.

(1994), "What do debt ratios tell about developing countries' economic futures?", *Journal of Economic Cooperation Among Islamic Countries*, 14:2.

(1997a), *Money in Islam*. London, England: Routledge.

(1997b), "The epistemologies of Ghazzali, Kant and the alternative: Formalism in unification of knowledge applied to the concepts of markets and sustainability", in J.C. O'Brien (ed.), Special Issue of *International Journal of Social Economics*, 24:7/8/9 (Lectures in Honour of Clement Allan Tisdell, Part III), 918–940.

(1998), *Reforming the Muslim World*. London, England: Kegan Paul International.

(2000), *The Islamic Worldview: Socio-Scientific Perspectives*. London, England: Kegan Paul International.

(2002), *Explaining the Qur'an: A Socio-Scientific Enquiry*. Lewiston, New York: The Edwin Mellen Press.

(2004), *The Islamic World-System: A Study in Polity-Market Interaction*. London, England: Routledge Curzon.

(2005), *Islamic Economics and Finance: Where Do They Stand?* Proceedings of the international conference on "Islamic Economics and Banking in the 21st Century", Jakarta, Indonesia, November.

(2006), *Science and Epistemology in the Qur'an* (different volume titles), 5 Vols. Lewiston, NY: The Edwin Mellen Press.

Choudhury, M.A. and Hoque, M.Z. (2004), *An Advanced Exposition in Islamic Economics and Finance*. Lewiston, NY: The Edwin Mellen Press.

Choudhury, M.A. and Hossain, M.S. (forthcoming 2007), *Computing Reality*. Tokyo, Japan: Aoishima Research Institute.

Choudhury, M.A. and Hussain, M. (2005), "The paradigm of Islamic banking", *International Journal of Social Economics*, 32:3, 203–217.

Choudhury, M.A. and Korvin, G. (2002), "Simulation versus optimization in knowledge-induced fields", *Kybernetes: International Journal of Systems and Cybernetics*, 31:1, 44–60.

Choudhury, M.A., Zaman, S.I. and Al-Nassar, Y. (forthcoming 2007), "A knowledge-induced operator model", *Sultan Qaboos University Journal of Science*.

Dampier, W.S. (1961), *A History of Science and Its Relations with Philosophy and Religion*. Cambridge, England: Cambridge University Press.

Darwin, C. (1859, 1936), *Descent of Man* (also known as *The Origin of Species*). New York, NY: Modern Library.

Dasgupta, A.K. (1987), *Epochs of Economic Theory*. Oxford, England: Basil Blackwell.

Dawkins, R. (1976), *The Selfish Gene*. New York: Oxford University Press.

Debreu, G. (1959), *Theory of Value: An Axiomatic Analysis of Economic Equilibrium*. New York, NY: John Wiley.

Dewitt, B. (1992), *Supermanifolds*. Cambridge, England: Cambridge University Press.

Feiwel, G.R. (1987), *Arrow and the Foundation of the Theory of Economic Policy*. London, England: Macmillan.

Fischer, S. (1997), "Capital account liberalization and the role of the IMF", *IMF Staff Paper*, September.

Friedman, M. (1989), "Quantity theory of money", in J. Eatwell, M. Milgate and P. Newman (eds.), *The New Palgrave: Money*. New York: W.W. Norton.

Fukuyama, F. (1992), *The End of History and the Last Man*. New York: The Free Press.

Giddens, A.
    (1983a), *A Contemporary Critique of Historical Materialism, Vol. 1: Power, Property and the State* (particularly pp. 26–48). Berkeley, CA: University of California Press.
    (1983b), *Emile Durkheim: Selected Writings*. Cambridge, England: Cambridge University Press.

Godel, K. (1965), "On formally undecidable propositions of Principia Mathematica and related systems", in M. Davies (ed.), *The Undecidable*. New York: Raven Books.

Gruber, T.R. (1993), "A translation approach to portable ontologies", *Knowledge Acquisition*, 5:2, 199–200.

Halmos, P.R. (1974), *Measure Theory*. New York, NY: Springer-Verlag.

Hawking, S.W.
    (1988), *A Brief History of Time: From the Big Bang to Black Holes*. New York: Bantam Books.
    (2004), Hawking, S. lecture given at 17th International Conference on General Relativity and Gravitation, Dublin, Ireland, reported in *New Scientist*, 21st July. http://www.damtp.cam.ac.uk/strtst/dirac/hawking/

Hawley, A.H. (1986), *Human Ecology*. Chicago, IL: The University of Chicago Press.

Hegel, G.W.F. (1956), *The Philosophy of History*, Trans. J. Sibree. New York, NY: Dover Books.

Heidegger, M.
    (1962), *Being and Time*, Trans. J. Macquarrie and E. Robinson. Oxford, UK: Basil Blackwell.
    (1988), *The Basic Problems of Phenomenology*, Trans. A. Hofstadter. Bloomington and Indianapolis, IN: Indiana University Press.

Heilbroner, R.L. (1985), *The Nature and Logic of Capitalism*. New York: W.W. Norton.

Heisenberg, W. (1958), in R.N. Anshen (ed.), *Physics and Philosophy*. New York, NY: Harper and Brothers Publishers.

Heiskala, R. (2003), *Society as Semiosis*. New York, NY: Peter Lang.

Henderson, J.M. and Quandt, R.E. (1971), *Microeconomic Theory: A Mathematical Approach*. New York, NY: McGraw-Hill.

Hogg, R.V. and Craig, A.T. (1965), *Introduction to Mathematical Statistics*. New York, NY: The Macmillan Co.

Hudson, M. (1993), *The Lost Tradition of Biblical Debt Cancellations*. New York: Robert Schalkenbach.

Hudson, M. and Van De Mieroop, M. (eds.) (2002), *Debt and Economic Renewal in the Ancient Near East*. Baltimore: CDL Press.

Hull, D.L. (1988), "Science as a selection process", in *Science as a Process*, Chapter 12. Chicago, IL: The University of Chicago Press.

HUMAINE. (16 December 2003), http://emotion-research.net/ Members/KCL

Hume, D. (1992), "Of the understanding", in *Treatise of Human Nature*. Buffalo, NY: Prometheus Books.

Huntington, S.P.
(1993), "The clash of civilizations?" *Foreign Affairs*, 72:3, 22–49.
(1995), "Islamic civilization will clash with Western civilization", in P.A. Winters (ed.), *Islam: Opposing Viewpoints*, pp. 205–212. San Diego, CA: Greenhouse Press, Inc.

Husserl, E. (1965), *Phenomenology and the Crisis of Philosophy*, Trans. Q. Lauer, p. 155. New York: Harper and Row Publishers.

Ibrahim, B.A. (2005), "Poverty alleviation by Islamic banking finance to microenterprises (MEs) in Sudan: Some lessons for poor countries", in M.A. Choudhury (ed.), *Money and Real Economy*. Leeds, UK: Wisdom House.

Kahf, M. (1992), "Financing the public sector in an Islamic perspective", in S. Sattar (ed.), *Resource Mobilization and Investment in an Islamic Economic Framework*. Herndon, VA: International Institute of Islamic Thought.

Kant, I. (1949), "Critique of pure reason", "Critique of judgment", "Reason within the limits of reason", "Idea for a universal history with cosmopolitan content", in C.J. Friedrich (ed.), *The Philosophy of Kant*. New York, NY: Modern Library.

Khan, M.F. (1991), "Time-value of money and discounting in Islamic perspective", *Review of Islamic Economics*, 1:2, 21–33.

Khan, M.S. and Mirakhor, A. (1989), "The financial system and monetary policy in an open Islamic economy", *Journal of King Abdulaziz University — Islamic Economics*, 1:1.

Koistinen, O. and Biro, J. (eds.) (2002), *Spinoza: Metaphysical Themes*. Oxford, England: Oxford University Press.

Kuhn, T. (1970), *The Structure of Scientific Revolutions*. Chicago, IL: University of Chicago Press.

Latif, S. and Hasan, A. (2007), "Rise and fall of knowledge power: An in-depth investigation", *Humanomics*, 23:3.

Levine, D. (1988), *Needs, Rights and the Markets*. Boulder, CO: Lynne Rienner Publishers.

Lloyd, E.A. (1988), *The Structure and Confirmation of Evolutionary Theory*. New York and London: Greenwood Press.

Lutz, M. and Lux, K. (1988), *Humanistic Economics: The New Challenge*. New York, NY: The Bookstrap Press.

Lyotard, J.-F. (1984), *The Postmodern Condition*. Manchester, UK: Manchester University Press.

Maddox, I.J. (1970), *Elements of Functional Analysis*. Cambridge, England: Cambridge University Press.

Marcuse, H. (1989), "One dimensional man", in H.B. McCullough (ed.), *Political Ideologies and Political Philosophies*. Toronto, Ont.: Wall and Thompson.

Marmura, M.E. (1997), *The Incoherence of the Philosophers*. Provo, Utah: Brigham Young University Press.

Marx, K. (1969), *Das Kapital*, Vols. 1–3. Frankfurt, Germany: Ullstein Verlag.

Masud, M.K. (1994), *Shatibi's Theory of Meaning*. Islamabad, Pakistan: Islamic Research Institute, International Islamic University.

Mathur, P.N. (1977), "A study of sectoral prices and their movements in British economy in an input-output framework", in W. Leontief (ed.), *Structure, System and Economic Policy*. Cambridge, UK: Cambridge University Press.

McCloskey, D.N. (1985), *The Rhetoric of Economics*. Wisconsin, Minnesota: The University of Wisconsin Press.

Mommsen, W.J. (1998), "Weber's life", in *The Political and Social Theory of Max Weber*, pp. 3–23. Chicago, IL: The University of Chicago Press.

Myrdal, G. (1977), "Institutional economics", Lecture at the University of Wisconsin, 15 December. Reprinted in his *Essays and Lectures After 1975*, Kyoto, Japan: Keibunsha.

O'Donnell, R.M. (1989), "Epistemology", in *Keynes: Philosophy, Economics and Politics*, pp. 81–105. London, England: Macmillan.

Penrose, R. (1989), *The Emperor's New Mind*. Oxford, England: Oxford University Press.

Phelps, E.S. (1985), *Political Economy*. New York: W.W. Norton.

Popper, K.R. (1972), *Conjectures and Refutations: The Growth of Scientific Knowledge*. London, England: Routledge and Kegan Paul.

Prigogine, I. (1980), *From Being to Becoming*. San Francisco, CA: W.H. Freeman.

Resnick, S.A. and Wolff, R.D. (1987), *Knowledge and Class: A Marxian Critique of Political Economy*. Chicago, IL: The University of Chicago Press.

Robbins, L. (1935), "The nature of economic generalizations", in *An Essay on the Nature and Significance of Economic Science*. London, England: Macmillan Press Ltd.

Russell, B.
   (1990), *A History of Western Philosophy*, pp. 756–765. London, England: Unwin Paperbacks.
   (2001), *The Problems of Philosophy*. Oxford, England: Oxford University Press.

Sauer, J. (2002), "Metaphysics and economy — the problem of interest: A comparison of the practice and ethics of interest in Islamic and Christian cultures", *International Journal of Social Economics*, 29:1&2, 97–118.

Schumpeter, J.A. (1961), *The Theory of Economic Development*, Trans. R. Opie. Cambridge, MA: Harvard University Press.

Schutz, A. (1970), *On Phenomenology and Social Relations: Selected Writings*. Chicago, IL: University of Chicago Press.

Shackle, G.L.S. (1971), *Epistemics and Economics*. Cambridge, England: Cambridge University Press.

Sherover, C.M. (1972), *Heidegger, Kant and Time*. Bloomington, IN: Indiana University Press.

Smith, T.S. (1992), *Strong Interactions*. Chicago, IL: University of Chicago Press.

Sztompka, P. (1991), *Society in Action: The Theory of Social Becoming*. Chicago, IL: The University of Chicago Press.

Thayer-Bacon, B. (2003), "Why (e)pistemology?" in *Relational (E)pistemologies*, pp. 14–48. New York: Peter Lang.

Tobin, J. (1958), "Liquidity preference as behavior towards risk", *Review of Economic Studies*, 26:1, 65–86.

Todaro, M.P. and Smith, S. (2005), *Economic Development*. Addison Wesley.

Ventelou, B. (2005), *Millennial Keynes*, Trans. P. Nowell. New York: M.E. Sharpe.

Wallerstein, I. (1998), "Spacetime as the basis of knowledge", in O.F. Borda (ed.), *People's Participation: Challenges Ahead*, pp. 43–62. New York: The APEX Press.

Zohar, D. and Marshall, I. (2004), *Spiritual Capital*. San Francisco, CA: Berrett-Koehler Publishers, Inc.

Index